THE RUSHY FIELD

by

SEÁN LOUGHRAN

Dedication

To kinsfolk Tommy, Pauline and Mary in Navan, Co. Meath
Liam and Cindy in Olympia, U.S.A.
Harry and Mary in Lathbury, Newport Pagnell,
Without whose faith and espousal these poems
might never have seen the light of day.

And specially to Tom Loughran, steam-engine
organiser, midnight-oil editor, proof-reader, and
perceptive commentator.

And not least to my wife Christine
who held the castle and kept the wheels turning
while I was less usefully engaged.

ABOUT THE AUTHOR

I spent most of my life learning, teaching, and half-forgetting the French language and I've written a few short stories - and told a lot of long ones - but I never wrote a line of verse until after my retirement.

Eventually, after kilograms of shredded paper I seemed to have tapped into some kind of artesian basin - one of the advantages of having had a long life - and, up to the moment, the waters still come gurgling up from time to time.

What do I write about? Almost anything but I find ideas in memories of the past, in relationships, in places far and near, in the "faith that looks through death" as my friend Willy Wordsworth once said, and, sadly, in a sense of outrage at the injustices, follies, brutalism and artistic depravity of our modern world. But, by contrast, I have an irrepressible sense of humour and frivolity and am thankful because in my verses I have found it possible – all too easy, in fact - to laugh at myself.

I like to think that those who read this book whether near or far, numerous or few, will find in it hope, consolation, amusement, vision, and even, most precious of all, the gift of tears. But I enjoyed writing these poems and that's what really matters in the first instance. To write poetry just for money is foolishness. And to think that anyone, except yourself, can teach you to write poetry is delusion.

Seán Loughran, 7th June 2009.

ABOUT THIS BOOK

This collection contains about 70 poems extremely diverse in style and treatment from the mysticism of "The Wild White Rose", to the frivolity of "Delph Dogs", from the coarseness of "Injury Time" to the harmonies of "Wild Wanton Wheat", from the vision of "One Moment Green" to the indignation of "My Singing Bird" etc. The poem "Legion" attempts to dramatise the complexity and contradictions that may be found in such diversities and in our genetic history.

Most of these poems are founded in my own personal experiences as a child in Belfast, as an evacuee in Co. Tyrone in 1941, in my travels in France and America, and in more familiar places like Strangford, Dunluce, Lecale, and most especially the Mountains of Mourne.

Many of the poems are narrative in character but they may also include the expression of some belief or reproach. "The Frugal Meal" is a consideration of the way in which so many of us overeat in a world where our forebears had so little. Included also are three long ballads, "Tristan Dubois" (a French officer who landed with Humbert in Mayo in 1798), "Omaha Flynn" (the Irish Famine, the American West and the misdeeds of General Custer), and a new rendition of "The Children of Lir".

A recurrent theme is the courage and integrity of the ordinary people of Belfast, qualities that persist though obscured by recent history. "Ode to a Doffer" was written in praise of all those who toiled in the mills and factories, the foundries and brickyards. Their graves are unmarked but their names are known in heaven as must surely be the names of the poor and destitute who are buried in innumerable graves in Milltown and other cemeteries.

Few of these poems can claim to be realistic. There is always more concern with the inner world that conflates memory, observation and desire.

"By Lagan Stream where lilies bloom,
I loved the Lady of Shalott
Though sigh of sedge, high toss of plume
Kept telling me that she was not".

A few spiritual verses have been inserted. Perhaps they illustrate the saying that poets rush in where angels fear to tread.
Romantic love – seen from a distance – is also included.
I was told that on this subject there is nothing new to be said. I have attempted to belie that statement.
Finally, as a kind of farewell or envoi, is the Poem "Birthday" which records the sorrows and satisfaction of reaching an eightieth anniversary and still paddling on.

"Where are they now, companions that walked the earth with me,
That knew the famine of the stars, the thirst that is the sea?"

Where indeed?

INDEX

THE RUSHY FIELD

In fathers' name, I'll sing a rushy field,
Wild-walled by blackthorn and the fierce dog-rose,
Undug, undrilled by spoiler's hand,
Dark hills beyond, where planners may not wield
Their ruffian writ to ravage and command.

A rushy field that knows nor plough nor spade,
Where larks ascendant from ogival grass
Translate the glories of a cornflower sky,
A field where hounded creatures sleep in shade,
A plot no predator shall rectify.

My banished people lacked most things that tillage yields.
The dairy and the grange became their foreign ground.
They scraped survival from bare slopes above.
But learned in time to love their tufted fields,
And, rhythmic by rushlight, transmit that guardian love.

BY TRASSEY BURN

Foam-ruffed and moiré-shawled, the streamlet seemed to say,
Mind those, short-lived as you, that passed this way,

Mat-headed hunters poising spears of stone,
Shore-dwellers from the antlered Viking flown,

Old ousted Gaels upon their trail of woe,
Wild ones that fled all toil and drudge below,

Grave mystics striving for the heights of prayer,
Packmen with Hollands gin for Hilltown fair,

Pilgrims, some glacial slab their penance bed,
Frenetics of the proud, the youthful tread,
Stone cutters, drovers, pot-still men -

You, too, may be remembered when
Cascading now is swept to then.

Chemised in shimmered silk, the stream shall say,
Who was he, then, that seldom day,
That scanned his verses as he passed my way?

SAHARA

I knew a man enamoured of the sand,
His inorganic world, dust rivers, no-green land,
Ice-meadows of the stars, rock-hammer sun,
He wove a tale whose warp I strove to understand.

In Ahaggàr by heat and hunger cursed,
(The blood, they say, is jellified by thirst)
He kneeled to kiss some foul and viscous pool,
And supped of camels' milk his rancid first.

The griddle of the hamada he knew,
Old shark-fin mountains where old ghost winds blew,
Black-shadowed sickles of the wandering dunes,
Shale plains, veiled tribes, heart-wrench adieu.

"It was his youth, monsieur", his uncle said.
"The springtime of his love, his thirst, his dread,
A paradise where scorpions sought his bed.
Sahara was a flame he thought to wed."

The sludge beneath the salt-pan crust that gulps the traveller down,
The muffling cagoule of the storm in which a man may drown,
I wondered then, I wonder now, if he was wise or mad,
To wring from torment sought, endured, such reason to be glad.

But sands of youth he shall not see again.
Nor I the morning fields of Aquitaine.

WILD WANTON WHEAT

Wild, wanton wheat,
In upland plot,
You whisper sweet,
Of what is not.

Wild, weathered wheat,
In wind and rain.
Sad, striving wheat,
For slender gain.

And shall you fade,
Unreaped, unknown?
No hiss of blade,
Where none has sown?

Or shall one bring,
Sandstone and hook,
Remembering,
What he forsook?

And shall he bend,
With scythe and stone,
Fulfil some end,
No, not your own?

Your clouded sky,
Is blank as snow,
Small field on high,
Where old winds blow.

Wild, wayward wheat,
In mountain plot,
Forgotten wheat,
Forget me not.

DEATH OF A COUNTRYMAN

He was as worn a man as I have seen,
Furrowed by age, leached as a harvest field,
The shrunken remnant of some former self,
That once gave battle to the deathless earth.

Above his bed, green peak and glen
Betrayed the fumbling labours of his heart.
Supine, he scarcely seemed to know
The dark from day, hubbub from time to sleep.

But, riffling through the chapbook of the years, he would declaim
Fragmented ballads, quaverings of song,
Of thrush and flowery dell and silver stream,
Of lovely maidens barefoot on the grass,
That bruised the heart and vision-fled away,
As, manful, he strode forth at break of day.

He seemed to doze; alarm was heard, by then
It was too late.
A lamp whose oil was done, the man went out.
The nurses bustled round, the matron rapped commands.
They had procedures, things-that-must-be-done.
The porters came.
The night staff slipped about
With cups of tea and prozac words.

The man that took his bed was young,
Expected well to live, subscribed to cocksure worlds,
Could not have known
Townlands that loved the sustenance of rhyme,
Or men that tinkered verses as they roamed
The long dark roads from home to home,
Or beauties trancing in the firelight's glow,
To throbbing airs of Aprils long ago.

We do not die complete,
We leave behind
A valuing, a world.

THE HATCHET FIELD

From tangle of Belfast it may be seen,
The Hatchet Field upon Black Mountain crest,
Triangle, point, long haft of green,
To urban view, proud symbol and bequest.

Once was a house of whitewashed stone, a byre,
Flood-run and path that angled up the hill,
Infrequent woodsmoke of some meagre fire,
Tall trees through which torrential airs would spill.

I ranged, one time, the heathers far and wide.
But keepers of the grass I seldom saw.
Mine was the brief embracement of the wild.
Its conquest was their mission and their law.

On destitution's edge, how did they live,
Disdaining pleasures of the world below?
Forlorn and raw, what could the wasteland give?
What recompense one fireless night of snow?

I skimmed the hilltops then, ran far and free,
Though now, from jolt and jostle, find a hymn,
Look up, look high, and standstill moments see,
Illumination on Black Mountain rim.

Could I ascend with friendship, feast and wine,
(For, time reversed, such marvels well may be)
In harmonies of flame that trip and twine,
We'd talk of clouds and cows and poetry.

They'd ply me with their vintage of content,
With singing of the wind, with mirth of brook,
Calligraphy of field their testament,
The city's million stars their picture book.

THE KING'S GRAVE

That mystic morn of May, how bold
And booted would I stoutly stray,
By Clonachullion Hill, Luke's Mountain, Slievenabrock.
Yet, still, in forest tongue where shadows lay,
I was induced to pause, to linger, and to stay.

Do you remember that your cairn of stone
Became, that livelong day, my megalithic throne?

Steep bluebell fields, afar, around, close by,
Took sheen and shimmer from a fleece-gold sky,
Sad swish and sift of pine wished requiem,
From sluice and swirl deep Shimna made reply.

Your kindred toiled to raise this memento.
Could they, so much as you and I,
Have loved these mountains so?

In quietude of murmur of the trees,
I saw you rest, a chieftain at his ease,
Before a jig of flame, your weapons cast aside,
Your sturdy children happy as the breeze.

Their short-lived laughter filled the air.
(Small, screeching spirits, swifting there.)

On such a day and in this selfsame sun,
When frost and rule of charnel night were done,
When summer, crowned with whin, from springtime sprang,
Then all your people gathered, feasted, sang,
And round you danced as mountain rivers run.

Now, clenched in blackness, all alone?
Corroded chain? Time-eaten bone?

Slow swing of treetops soothed the rooks to sleep.
It was the hour
When shadows from abyss of earth uprise to weep.

I left the place where once a king
Had seen his evening close.
I left the place where now a king
Dwells in his long repose . . .

But do you mind that I did stay,
King, druid, bard, that single day?

"OMAHA FLYNN"

In 1994 when I was roamin' in Wyomin', I fell over this old rapscallion who offered to sell me an authentic tin bugle which his grandpappy had won after the battle of the Little Bighorn in 1876.

I pointed out the fact that the bugle had been made in China and looked almost new, but as soon as I admitted I was from Ireland, the red-haired hustler announced that his name was Firewater Flynn and launched himself into this Niagara-type narrative about the epic adventures of his grandaddy who didn't seem to know the difference between America and Ireland, between Cromwell and Custer, or even between truth and fiction.

I didn't believe him, of course. I mean, the whole story was a welter of cliché, myth and brass-necked bull and, just for a start, the village on the Washita where Custer enjoyed his genocidal games was inhabited by the Cheyenne and not by the Sioux to whom the original Omaha Flynn was supposed to have become affiliated.

Still, the story, as well as being worth a pint of bourbon, exerted and continued to exert its own weird fascination so that, like the Ancient Mariner, I was compelled to break free by reducing it to verse and passing it on, as now, to some simple soul or souls even more credulous than myself. But you must read the poem **for entertainment only**. It isn't a history lesson. In fact, I'll let you into a secret. The key word to the whole thing is in the second-last line. And it isn't "buffalo".

P.S. I was back in the same one-horse town a week later and I heard the old buzzard telling an innocent tourist and his wide-eyed wife that Omaha Finnborg was Swedish.

Seán Loughran 1st April 2009

THE BALLAD OF OMAHA FLYNN

I am a scion of the Flynn
A fearless and ferocious clan.
Heroic was our origin,
We faced the Viking, man to man.

I am descended of the Flynn,
From storied fields of Kilcolman.
We stormed his castle, burst it in,
Poor poet Spenser skipped and ran.

My father's father worked a forge.
He hammered pikes in Ninety-Eight.
The cavalry of Good King George,
They flogged and hanged him at his gate.

The Yeos pitch-capped my granda Doyle
(Such playful teasings kept them happy)
And when his brains began to boil,
They mocked - they aped - the Dancing Croppy.

My father was a highwayman,
He parleyed with our Saxon masters,
Post-haste to Dublin town they ran,
Lamenting loudly their disasters.

The Redcoats strutted round Fermoy
In gleaming brass and silver chain.
My father doffed his hat with joy
To think of those that he had slain.

"I give you now, me fine bucko,
Two silver pistols worth the prizin',
Their owner in the bog below,
His crimes preventin' him from risin'"

Outcasts in our dear land of birth
Like rapparees or ancient tories,
We tenemented on the earth,
Enraptured by the minstrels' stories.

And I mind the deeds of Finn McCool,
And the Wild Geese southward flyin',
And the tales of Ireland's long misrule,
And Sarsfield vainly dyin'.

But the curse of Cromwell fell once more,
Upon our tattered, tortured land,
Where Hunger, driven out of door,
Consumed dead things upon the strand.

Roast beef and pudding for their tea,
Our praties black and rotten.
They laughed with glee, we soon would be
Rare as the Huron in Manhattan.

My father died, my mother too,
I roved the rambling roads in the rain.
I sold the pistols, well I knew
I wasn't returning again.

And I cursed and I cried upon that day,
I boarded a barque for Amerikay . . .

That ship was an eternal Hell,
Though many from it were released,
The boom of wave their funeral knell,
The ballast man their surly priest.

They dumped us on some crowded dock,
Their hungry cities sucked us in.
Bemused by sickness, sorrow, shock,
We were the prey of fraud and sin.

Those swarming slums I could not stand,
 Sad fringes for those stranded masses.
I had to reach the open land,
 Unsullied skies, uncharted grasses.

On a horse I bought for English gold,
I travelled far, I travelled bold.

Old moon, that shone on Aherlow,
You see me by the Ohio.

I journeyed far as man might dare,
Years, rivers, mountains, prairies, flowed.
I disremember why or where,
I took the outlaws' crooked road.

I rode with Ed and Jack L'Estrange,
McCoy and Dillon, Memphis too.
We robbed the stagecoach and the trains.
The whiskey poured, the dollars flew.

"I carry this couple of Paterson Colts,
There's nothing you'll dare to deny me.
I hold in these pistols twelve thunderbolts,
And only a fool would defy me."

The Owl Hoot Trail was our shibboleth.
But the owl is a bird that sings of death . . .

This lad, one day, in Wichita,
He fired upon me from behind.
His aim was bad, swift was my draw.
He lived - recovered - and was blind.

Alone, I rode the wagon trails,
Their broken wheels my only fuel,
And found in coyotes' heartsick wails
Some strange and deep and mad renewal . . .

Between the painted tents we wended,
Walled in by each unsmiling face.
He spoke - the hunter I'd defended -
I found a nation and a place.

I chose to stay and not to go,
I bought into their way of life,
This wildness that I seemed to know,
I found a people and a wife . . .

Once and forever mountain glades,
Spired spruce, sweet seasons, mirrored water.
Dark as the velvet night your braids.
We have two sons, a blue-eyed daughter.

My woman of the Western Sioux.
My hearth . . .   My flame . . .
My Roisin Dubh . . .

With bow of ash and knife of stone
I raced upon a thundering tide.
With buffalo the plains were strown.
Food, shelter, weapons, robes of hide.

Upon their bellies in the grass,
They killed from over half a mile.
The fattened plains where they had passed
Blushed bloodlust, famine, greed and guile.

The hungry children cried for more.
This was a sound I'd heard before . . .

Our chief rode out in all his pride,
Hawk-feathered banner, eagle bonnet.
"You lousy savage!", Custer cried,
"You can take yourself to hell or - Connaught!"

Discarded dolls upon the snows . . .
My sons . . . My Singing Bird . . .
My Small Dark Rose . . .

Red, red, as berries on the haw.
When Custer came to the Washita.

          The cries I cried, I cry them still . . .

In the horns of my sacred buffalo,
And my breastplate of porcupine quill.
I took the soldier's Springfield gun.
For life - for land to come and go -

This was a fight that must be won.

Cheyenne and Sioux in fierce array,
We swept the field, we won the day.

For Crazy Horse, that gallowglass,
He covered our names with lustre.
He led us over the Greasy Grass,
And we settled that bastard Custer.

Cheyenne and Sioux in fierce array,
We lost the war, we won the day . . .

     *   *   *   *   *   *

"Now, boys, we gottus this renegade.
We'll fetch us a rope an' have us some fun."
My Colts were loaded, I wasn't afraid.
I dropped them around me, dead every one.

A mile or two more, then I fell in the sand.
The brave animal knelt down beside me.
I saved the last bullet, he died by my hand.
Come evenin', the hungry wolves eyed me.

The mists weave around me, my days are all spent,
The night wind seems colder and colder.
The pain it is gone but them wolves are hell-bent
To make certain I don't get no older . . .

To see again my Small Dark Rose,
My children and my kinsmen too,
And all the people of the Sioux,
My knife I loose, my eyes I close.

For in that Happy Hunting Ground,
All we have loved and lost is found . . .

        We pitch our tepees down below
        The long-lost vale of Aherlow . . .

        And kill the crazy buffalo,
        In that green land where shamrocks grow . . .

THE WILD WHITE ROSE

The stanchions of the gate were nibbled bone.
The rusted links of chain in tangles lay.

Enclosed in stillness of the fields,
I crossed a stile, its sandstone scooped
By long remembrance, heart's return,
Traversed the hawthorn's fallen snow,
Attained the place where many slept,
Unmoved by thrust of bracken, briar, and spray,
Unstirred by seethe of sap and blood,
Unroused by call of bird, by gladness of the day.

Then, all too soon, some anger came, I bled to see
The fettle of those happy living things,
Their warm impulse of joy, their wholeness, self-content,
That shut me out as, mortal, I perceived
Some symphony of nature, canticle of May,
Some quietude of being far above our thought,
Some concert that outlives our mortal fray.

I will not tour the tombs, I thought, nor read the names,
Nor scan the chiselled testaments of love and faith,
Nor tot the cold arithmetic of death,
Nor wander in the shade of that voracious night,
Nor link reflection to our common doom.

That said, I lingered in some undefined desire,
In contemplation of that mystery unresolved,
That gulf that lay between those flawless things above,
And those, unseen, that melted far below.

This seemed a wrong that must outrange the mind,
And poison all contentment of the heart, and then,
In moment of unlooked-for grace,
I saw the rose, the wild white rose,
That grew above a sag of clay,
Where earth to earth, embracing, lay.

I neared the rose, and then and there it seemed
That all were one,
What had been, was, and was ordained to be,

That vested now with higher things,
Those quiet folk that tilled their furrows once,
That fructified the earth, that broke the sod,
New artisans of promise, those and those
Green-glossed the grass, made bright the weed,
And white as christening robe the wild white rose

GREAT STONE OF ARDARA

Asperged by ocean spray, the rock
Its lichens, moons, cloud-fringe of gold,
Its saturation, script, its hieroglyphs, these
May be, or are, divulgence of a kind.

Such things I see,
Sea-orphaned pools, small flowers that sway
In ecstasy or pain,
The sadness of the ebbing tide . . .
But cold, in reach of hand, a language that I cannot read,
A manuscript I never shall decode,
A chart by which I may not navigate
On any mortal sea.

Some cowl-grave scholar from the voids of time,
Immersed in recondite and pious lore,
Might scan these patterns, put this stone to rhyme,
Retrieve therefrom a science heard no more.

Or barefoot hermit from his mossy den,
Attuned to silence and to awful thought,
Could pore upon this text, discovering then
Epiphany in sacred fury sought.

Or minstrel that would haunt this final strand,
To catch the notion of its urgent spell,
Might, by the scorings of this stonework, stand,
To pluck in strings the mysteries they may tell.

But scholar, hermit, minstrel, I am not their peer.
My verse dissolves, I linger and
This living fresco still evades, great stone of Ardara,
For all the gist and burden of its runes,
Is dense, impregnable, embraces close
Its secrecies.

Yet grace and gladness it is now to know,
That there is meaning here, was governance and plan,
And Word that was before the clay began.

THE ABSTRACT LABRADOR

From prattling picture and fictitious woe,
The man reviewed, five miles below,
His bleak, antique, his loveless Labrador.

An aimless scrawl, a daub, a random poem,
Of fjord and lake and rock in monochrome,
Familiar and so far, the abstract Labrador.

Uncut by road, untouched by human hand,
White-wrinkled hills, snow marches, glacial sand,
Depressed by altitude, the cruel Labrador.

Congealing seas beset by frost and floe,
Stone-stippled tundra where black-spruce winds blow,
His ancient, ice-love, achromatic Labrador.

By lemon grove, or vineyard hill,
In air-conditioned mall, it haunted still,
His shadowing, his wolf-pack Labrador.

By Judas tree or cactus floor,
Cold was the place he'd known before,
His ever and pursuivant Labrador.

KILLOUGH

BRIGHT . . .
I remember Bright.
Deep-drowsed, peep-housed, sleep-soused in light,
Fields estivating in long, lush and leafy light,
Maze-meadows, buttercupped in doze and dream,
Unroused

By clash of carriage door,
By scream of steam,
Chug-tugs, metallic clanks.

BRIGHT . . . farewell . . . .

Glad grind of brakes, such scramble and commotion ! !
At last, at longing last, the station at Killough ! ! !
Nasturtiums -
Spurred, punchinello-yellow, nose-clown red,
And red-hot pokers in the sun ! ! !
(Mother Nature's splendid fun.)

Arrived in jubilee,
June jigs upon the inner harbour and in silver fire
Boats bob and dip and nod and know
That, gleeful, we would come to this -

This coin-bright-minted world inventing joys for boys,
 Thrill tints of shell and shingle, lichened crags,
Toy textures, tastes and fantasies,
Rib-rippled sand, wave-polished-soup-tin-sinking stones,
Thin shards of slate for water hop-and-skim,
Sour sun-steamed kelp in canyons of the shore,
Tongue-scorching dulse for changing water into wine,
Green globes of glass that knew the stormy brine,
Pan-sizzling summer herrings fleshed like cream,
Mint-breathing marsh-weed on the fringe of Munce's Lough,
Sand-hoppers' prance on Saint-Helena's beach,
Aloft-alarm of gulls to pierce each dawn-dull head . . .
Beyond the quiet church, the cornfields splashed with red . . .

Such eagerness to learn

The marvel of the tides that we might know
Their sink and surge, and follow for a blessed time
Their solemn ritual of ebb and flow.

In pink and sun-meshed paddling pools, anemones
Shall kiss our fingertips cold welcome. Limpets
Happy as besotted lovers on a string
Shall woo the goofy mollygowans to
Their jampot destiny. Chivalrous crabs
Emergent to their parabolic glory
Shall stoic-soar from catapult of arm,
The spotted fluke
Wrenched flapping from its warm and gritty bed
Shall feel our blacksmith barb as ecstacy.

Outside the forge
Farm horses wait
To do their stampy sparky stenchy tingly turn.
Oh, singe-hoof smell, oh, clang of anvil bell!
Here, shortcuts, stiles,
The stump on Windmill Hill, grasshopper-ticking Rossglass Road,
Shall all rejoice for us . . .

This country was, we thought, a feast for nimble lads.
We had not known
The burden of the siren's song,
The tonnage of romance,
Nor known
This world would turn, would turn,
Upon a spindle of its own.

This was, for sure, a carousel
Where joy was ever twirling, twirling fast.
For all that lived and breathed, this Eden held
Creation's morning bright.

It must have been such sport to waltz
Upon the dancing-floor of summer seas,
Haul in the silver treasures of the sea,
Puff tin-roofed pipe of clay upon a three-legged stool,
Swop salt-and-sea-dog tales around a driftwood fire,
Or step, blue-ganseyed, sun-burned ship-ahoy,
Beneath the sycamores of Carman's Row
Or, tranquil, toss horseshoes fornent the Chapel Brae.

Most envied too . .
The railwaymen with their prodigious toys,
The engine-drivers black as Abyssinian kings,
The stokers streaming with their epic sweat,

And, envied too
The station staff that surely knew
The secrets of the chocolate-bar machines,
And played leap-frog on churns of milk,
By mad and merry moonbeam light,
When, day and night, the world was bright.

It was quite clear, the thought was dear,
That all were safe, sure-sure and ever-glad,
Dear-dwelling in Killough from year to year.

Once, once, I ventured to return, I saw
Rank graveyards, nettled, nourished, hungry still.
An ageing man with distant gaze who was perhaps
Among the crowd long, long ago,
That sang The Quartermaster's Store upon the pier . . .

I wonder if he was perhaps the one
That dived head-first from off the end,
To thwart, when currents raged, the swelling tide,
And cartwheel on the farther shore,
While squealing girls acclaimed his hateful might.

I'd best not ask.
That better man he may not be.
He may be one of those that shrank like me,
And came to dread in that last year
The surge and cyclones of a newfound sea.

MY SINGING BIRD

I've seen the lark soar high at morn -

> From chevrons of the grass he sprang.
> The land rejoiced, the heavens rang.

To sing up in the blue -

> Thon gulpin nested in my field,
> When nothin' mattered barrin' the yield.

I've heard the blackbird pipe his note -

> He'll sing no more upon my tree,
> Nor trespass on my property.

The thrush and the linnet too -

> Results! Results! Our lan' was sprayed.
> Thon unproductive pests are dead.

But none of them can sing so sweet -

> But none of them will sing at all,
> Nor make my farmin' incomes fall.

My singing bird as you.

> Stay in your cage, my cockatoo,
> There, hopefully, they won't get you.

ODE TO A DOFFER

"I wish I was married and out of the mill,
And had a wee house on top of the hill."
  (Inscription seen on a wall in Odessa Street, Belfast.)

You hug the coat tightly around you,
Your head-scarf all sodden wi' sleet.
Old plimsolls your mammy has found you
Slip-slop in the slush of the street.

Late-late, young-old, ay, bone-weary,
You ply to the will of the mill,
Though, deep down, a dream held so dearly,
A wee house on the top of the hill.

The horn to your horror is moanin',
And these are the words that are said,
"You'll labour in loss and in groanin',
Until you are done for or dead."

Affright and a-flounder this mornin',
You know from that long brazen bray,
That the gates may be shut without warnin',
No use then to plead or to pray.

But the gateman, an' here's a real wonder,
He meets you, for once, wi' a grin.
An' to stragglers he roars like the thunder,
"Come on on, yiz hoors! Get yiz in!"

I'll not enter those cells of constriction.
Far better the wind and the sleet.
I'll step back from those halls of affliction.
Far safer the cold of the street.

I daren't go, wee Rose, where you're yearnin'.
I'd faint in the heat an' the smell.
There's death in the shillin's you're earnin'.
You're deep in warm waters of hell.

You toil in a turmoil of clatter,
A world where discussion is mute,
Where machines to each other may chatter,
But humans are dumb as the brute.

From heavens bruise-black and smoke-dreary,
Soot snowflakes that fall on the mills.
Inside, heart-scalded an' weary,
You breathe the white powder that kills.

The spindles spin swift as a lifetime,
Keep goin', wee Rosie, but still
You'll dream of the better, the wife-time,
That wee house on the top of the hill.

But a pause now, a whistle, a slowin',
A silence that hums in the ear,
A smilin', a laughin', a goin',
A bustle, a push and a cheer.

Forget now, wee Rosie, the chokin',
An' the fibres that clot in your chest.
Forget that you're wringin' an' soakin'.
Just caper an' sing with the rest.

The doffers link elbow to elbow,
An' swing till the end of the street.
They sing like the sun on the rainbow.
An' God help the fellas they meet.

"FAN-A-WINNOW - A - E - O.
FAN-A-WINNOW, DAISY!"

Fan-a-winnow, - a - e - o.
Fare ye well, wee Rosie.

They were rough, they were rude, they were cheeky and their language was choice. But they were the salt of the earth. My best poem will always be the one I haven't written yet. But this, to me, is my second best.

DUNLUCE

Come see this limpet fortress at the world's wet end,
Incised, trepanned, by surgeon wind and wave,
Touch mortared walls of old volcanic stone,
Strong-held in times quite murderous as our own.

Descend with care slip-slopes, then contemplate
Slime-bouldered bore-hole, hear sea-slosh and moan.
Ascend to banquet hall where minstrels played.
Survey drowned scullery, pace the colonnade.

Feel ocean breath spill down the quadrant world,
Poseidon whimper in his black arcade,
Sweep scene with mini-cam. Forget the carriageway.
Then choose to rest, to conjure, and to stay.

Lap up the fitful sun. This inner ward,
This cobbled yard stores glimmers of the day.
Hear muted growling of the wearied sea.
Enjoy such comfort as may seldom be.

Imagine anvil of the night, black bellows of the storm,
Mad sob and shriek of scalded-heart banshee.
Dream, as you drowse, of beaux and beauties past,
Of lord and village maid, high feast and humble fast.

Admire the modern privilege of your rest.
This place scoffed herd and harvest, gorged until the last,
Took wood and water, wasted friend and foe,
Drove men that drove dumb beasts in sleet and snow.

Look right, look long, on leaving by the bridge
On this green field unspaded now although
Here lived unlaurelled ones to build, defend
This mortal symbol of our world's dark end.

JACK AND JILL

Come with me, said Jack, to his halo-haired Jill,
By the slippery road that twists over the hill.
The primrose is faded, the bluebells are high.
In a green velvet cradle we'll pleasantly lie.

The streamlets are pure and the evening is sweet.
'Tis time that our love was fulfilled and complete.
From tapestried hollow don't send me away.
Brief is the rose blossom and short is the day . . .

Mischieving of Jack that has broken his crown,
Perceiving of lovers that, wiser, pass down,
Deceiving of lovers that know they will part,
And grieving of Jill that is breaking her heart.

THE DOLPHINS

El Nino did his stuff, we had
Five days, cold wind and rain.
The sun returned at length, the vines redressed.
Gold citrus gleamed in regimented files.
And half of California rushed to Waterworld.

All highways clogged, queues to the parking lot.
Long lines at every fast-food joint, at last
(Hell was the other people, not ourselves)
A seat in lower tiers beneath the blistering sun.

To cries of joy
The dolphins poked their circus snouts above
The pool. Snap-gobbled fish
And danced upon their tails, skipped backwards, played
Fit-fiddle children loosed from school.
They curved in air, parabolas of joy,
Splashed down in element more kin to them,
Than ours to us.
One raced, torpedo-like, wet gleaming steel,
A waving girl upon its back.
Oh, they were proud
Of what they'd learned or what they always knew.
The dolphins laughed
To leap and dive
To be alive.

One soared, leviathan, hung, grinned, and flopped
In liquid detonation, splash and spray.
I laughed with families of the land and of the sea.
I laughed to hear the squeak and twitter of the dolphins' play.
I smiled when someone said, wet-through like me,
"The dolphins have a sense of humour too."

Unanswered questions taunt me still.
For all we find, explain, expound,
Is there some innocence that they possess?
Integrity we lost or never found?
Are they amused by welter of our brain?
Are we, not they, the ones that entertain?

DISTRACTION

Most of the time, the most of us
Are in the balcony.
Cocooned, secure, bug-snug, aloft.

The Show, though vulgar, cheapjack, no great cop,
(The sound-effects primordial)
Gives no real reason for complaint.

We love to share their glitzy lives.
Those cheery stars we recognise,
Our Friends and Neighbours in the soaps,
That feed our covert dreams and hopes,

Festooned with trollops of delight,
The superstuds that shoot on sight,
Such rips and rascals, merry brutes,
And bumbling, lewd, Big-Bro galoots,

The cads, the cards, the Pharisees,
The OOOH! so naughty hes and shes,
Mad demagogues that rant and bray,
Politicos with feet of clay,

The guiding lights whose brains are dick,
The gastronomes that make us sick,
The simians that prance and bawl,
How well we know and love them all!

While, from their hebetating hell,
We slurp the message that they tell,
The Golden Rule that stay we should,
Ensconced in Dumb Beatitude,
Which, after all, is For Our Good.

It happens though,
The floor gives way
You fall
Into the Pit
Where there is blood and darkness, gangrene of the heart.

Too well, too deep, you then will know,
The reason why they wanted you
To concentrate upon
The Show.

JOE'S BIKE

I'd been expatriated long enough
To know the little townlands inside out,
To butterfly the hedges far and near,
To squirrel sky-piercing trees in primal woods,
Set hopeless snares the rabbits giggled at,
And gorge myself on depth-charge gooseberries,
And raspberries from midge-tormented bogs . . .

But never had I heard of Joe,
Suspected, even, his existence,
Until I tripped and almost fell
Over the lolling of his legs,
Protracted on the floor
Below the creaking sisters' stairs

While he scooped cold stew from a blackened pot,
Gulping and bolting like a hungry dog.

And there, within that proper hall,
Joe's bike was flung against the wall,
Quite heedless of propriety,
Or goggle-eyed evacuee.

I rubbed my eyes, and looked again, again.

An iron-rationed bike.
The perfect minimum of bike.
Stripped bare and disencumbered.
A lesson in subtraction.

A rusty frame.
Two wheels with spokes enough for one.
A handlebar south-west north-east.
An ad-lib chain.
No brakes,
No pedals, mudguards, pump or lights.
Nothing, nothing, **nothing**, needless.
Of life and limb this man was heedless.

A moment later, he was gone.
He stretched, and grinned, and lit a butt -
Was gone
Upon his bike

Whistling and slaloming down the brae.
Go-lucky-happy,
Gallant,
Free
From dull respectability
Upon his bike.
We twigged damn soon that gipsy Joe belonged
To that hospitable abode,
Where lodged, that time, our blitz-blown clan,
Where Sue and Sarah held their brief domain,
That age of Barbarossa and El Alamein,
Of wild and rustic joys that will not come again.

We saw Joe several times thereafter,
That summer that we spent in far Tyrone,
That unforseen and thaumaturgic season.
He landed, fed, lit up, was gone
Upon his bike.

That boyo works, said Sue, ah, wistful, sad,
For farmers when the notion takes him -
Which, God knows, isn't very often.

We never know just where that lad might be,
Confided Sarah, to her spudful spade,
He sleeps in haystacks, barns and ditches
All roun' the country, it's a terror, so it is.

You'd think he'd find some decent kind of job,
Said Solemn Sue.
The times are better than we ever knew.
The likes of Joe could make four pound-a-week or more.
(His trouble was, he never knew the score.)

A lifetime later - or almost -
I motored back to see,
The place that lived in hoarded memory.

Now Sue and Sarah and recumbent Joe,
Slept well in sumptuous plot, all three,
Invisible equality,
Where gormful and the gormless must agree.

Down in the local they talked on and on,
About the sisters and the family tree.

And what (I dared to ask) of Joe?

Ah, Joe, he died in 'Forty-Nine,
Below a bus on the Omagh line . . .

(Whistling and slaloming down the brae?)

And, still, I see him, rapparee,
Wheel-borne and free
From dull routine and hell-s-d
Upon his bike.

The sisters' lives were prudent, long, secure.
Joe's days were short, he lived complete.
He was the one I envied in my comfort.
My soft stravaigles never equalled his,
Nor paid his price,
Nor did I ever sleep beneath a hedge,
Nor share repose of unremembering beasts,
Nor burrow, deep in hay, beneath the cat's-eye stars.

Right now, I've got this bike of top design,
Shimano gears and alloy wheels,
And lamps, and phone to dial 999,
And vented helmet for my precious skull,
And I've been to California and to Tipperary too.

But I've never travelled half as far as Joe.
Nor relished such a stew.

NO SHADOWS NOW

By yonder road that straggles through my dream,
His geometric garden reigned supreme,
Infused with humming sun, idyllic with the rose,
And scented still beyond the long day's close.
Full often did we gape across leaf walls
(Blitzed ruffians from the Springfield and the Falls)
Or, playing war upon the neighbouring hill,
Lay down our hazel guns to marvel at his skill.

Yet, though the Master's flowers in ranks and squadrons grew
(One literary trooper termed them picture-skew)
Though tall delphiniums like guardsmen stood
To guard his childless solitude,
Congruent, marshalled, though his Eden was,
His Mastery was not complete because
His wanton lilacs revelled in the rain,
With scent so sweet that it was almost pain.
(While Panzers raced across the Russian plain.)

Each Sunday morning in the church,
The camphorated congregation stiffening in its stalls,
His Reverence intoned the solemn roll
Of those that had subscribed Parochial Dues.
The Master topped the list perforce,
Ex - as my uncle Fonsie said - officio,
Then came big farmers and the lesser folk below,
With fine distinction being made
Between the florins and the holy crowns,
And certain black sheep specified for having made, as yet,
No contribution.

This wasn't malediction, blast the thought,
It merely served to underline
The Seven Gifts
Of those who prayed and paid and little said,
And, all ungrudging, gave their lawful score,

Nor lurked in stingy gloom behind the door,
Who worked and gently cared till they could do no more.

He's in the shadow of the church, they said.
The day they buried him.
But, years afar,
The venerable church flew stone by stone away,
To be a Mass House in a Folk Museum.
(Such strange and final roundelay.)

The Master stayed
To Fortune and to Fame unknown,
And by his resting place a shadowed stone.

And later still,
They exorcised the ghost of Thomas Gray,
Did for the rugged elms, the yew-tree's shade,
The moping owl also,
For all I know.

Dark term complete,
His grave allures the splendour of the day.

Where he is now,
No shadows fall.

STRANGFORD LOUGH

Wheeling and whirring round the drumlin lands,
Green-apple hills of County Down,
I shuddered from, could not avoid
The sea.
Slung fences, eaten, undermined,
Weed sour and steaming in the sun.
(Blurred clouds of meadowsweet.)

Again, again, salt jabbings of the wave,
Enclosures gashed, green fields harpooned in sleep,
Scraped bones of rock, slime-lappings cold as blood
Of ones that, glut with plunder, sailed upon the ebb.

Cool meadows here, tall beech, fern-croziered shade,
Grey innocence of flocks,
Were promised ease.
I saw a stile that I might cross,
A decent track that ran along and up.

I cut the engine's humming song,
Leaned the Black Shadow, ticking as it cooled,
Against a wall with pennywort bedizened,
Sought cease in rustling sedge, sandpipers' lonely cries.

But Thought was there.
Its sweep and flood and flow,
Salt, serpentine,
Ferocious as
The longships from the sea.

THE BALLAD OF TRISTAN DUBOIS

Give not your life, young man, I pray,
To wild adventure, mad foray.
Small glory shall you find, young friend,
Until the long, long day shall end . . .

I sailed for Ireland long ago.
Céline, she wept upon the shore.
For love is sharpened much by woe -
She knew, she knew, we'd meet no more.

Thus, pain and parting may not cease,
Jusqu'à ce que la longue journée finisse . . .

We little knew the land we sought,
Its people or its pride.
But they would flock to us, we thought,
And we would conquer side by side.

For Liberty they'd hungered long,
Equality and Brotherhood.
Our Marseillaise would be their song,
Our guillotine their sharpest good.

My own half-brother with me came,
Our widowed father's dearest son,
Ill-fated brother, Jean by name,
His eighteenth summer scarcely run.

Confined within a narrow hold,
Men played for sous and not for gold.
Stout Humbert, fists behind his back,
Paced out an empire on the deck.

Long, long, they played at rouge et noir,
In shelter from the wind and wave.
I dreamed of Ile de France afar,
And of this land that we would save.

We set foot on Kilcummin Strand,
Our ships, white birds of Liberty.
Our kettledrums awoke the land,
Our trumpets sang of Ireland free.

The morning gleamed across the bay.
More clear than crystal glass, the sea.
Our grenadiers made bold display.
Mon pauvre Jean, he smiled at me.

Some welcomed us with fierce delight,
Who long had longed for what we bore,
For weapons in an even fight,
To set them free from shore to shore.

But some, unworthy, looked away,
And, barefoot, wrought, nor turned their head.
From den of clay they would not stray,
Nor sordid comfort of their bed.

Killala I remember well.
We danced around our foes.
With bayonets fixed and piercing yell,
We smashed the cowardly Yeos.

Blue tunics in that sprawl of death,
And one chasseur that spun and fell.
Some icy horror stopped my breath,
Some anguish that no words could tell.

"This is, mon frère, a trifling hurt,
 A theme for jest in years to come."
"Why does your life-blood, brother, spurt?
 Why have you cold as death become?"

We buried him beside some nameless track.
Kind Teeling's words I could not understand.
We onward marched and none but I looked back
While brimful winds bereavèd all the land'.

"Sore, sore, the path we stumbled o'er,
By Lahardaun and Nephin Glen.
No dawn, no glory, might restore
The brother I had loved till then.

Oh, love and loss, they cannot mend,
Until the long, long day shall end . . .

Beyond the town of Castlebar,
The King's battalions won the race.
They flew so fast, they fled so far,
That none could match their headlong pace.

We rallied to our leader's side,
He reined his steed with wondrous pride.
"Bravo, mes braves!" , Umberto cried,
"To Dublin Castle shall we ride!"

But English cannon well had fed
On disregarded Irish dead. . .

Then, many swore in frenzied feast,
 This broken people would arise,
That, led by lord, asperged by priest,
Long-cherished dreams they'd realise.

But, Calm and Reason men forget,
They hunger after Vengeance yet.
And fearful things did Tristan see
About the Tree of Liberty.

Blood-blackened pikes, so long denied,
Green banners on a howling tide.
"Quels sont ces primitifs?" I cried.
"My countrymen", proud Teeling sighed.

"Viens, mon ami, you soon shall hear.
 Such notes as must enchant your ear.
Tho' thus by savage laws contrived,
These have endured, these have survived."

This Memory with life shall blend
Until this endless day shall end.

Bewitchment in that flick'ring night
Of dispossession's sorest wrong,
Wild faces seen in red firelight
By soldier silent in that throng,
By grenadier that's lived too long . . .

They echo still in midnight dream,
Those tones that sobbed along, along,
In voice more pure than silver stream.
For me alone she sang her song.

Deep-shadowed face beneath her shawl,
Harp strings that moaned with sorrow's skill,
Sweet vagrant words I still recall,
Sore-wounding air that haunts me still.

She sang, it seemed, of endless youth,
Upon some fabled shore,
Some blessèd land, more true than truth,
Where loss and longing are no more . . .

That Melody shall never cease,
Jusqu'à ce que là longue journée finisse . . .

The morning ashes shivered cold.
Bedraggled Humbert angry grew.
They had decamped that were so bold,
The brave that rested, far and few.
Our wakened sergeants stamped and swore,
Found here a handful, there a score.
Their leaders roared them into line.
Some rueful smiled, some glared malign.

"Those ragamuffins!" Humbert cried,
"Pour ces gens-là, your brother died?"
"Mon général, I cannot say,
What honour or what love has made them stay."

Nor, truth, I could not tell in days to come
What ancient, stubborn courage drove them on
Across the gulf of language they were dumb.
No words could tell what dreams they fed upon.

Unversed in war, I mused, why must they fight?
In tattered rags, why stumble to their tomb?
What chance, that they may vanquish England's might?
What naked steel, what rope, shall be their doom?

But, grenadiers, chasseurs, dragoons on borrowed steeds,
Took reassurance in our victories past,
For we had shattered kingdoms by our deeds,
And seen great armies reel from us aghast.

Our fleets, we thought, had swept the western sea.
Brave Hardy and Kilmaine would surely come.
The troops that won Arcole and Rivoli
Marched now, proud banners high, to Revolution's drum.

We'd crossed the Alps with Bonaparte,
His lightning stroke, his lion's heart . . .

His lion's heart, his lightning stroke -
Humbert recoiled. His courage broke.

Milord Cornwallis played the hound,
We turned our backs in shameful flight.
Ten English armies closed around,
Behind, ahead, to left, to right.

Through many a black and bitter scene,
We passed, sad omens of our venture's close,
By ruined cabins where no life was seen,
And gallows marked the mischief of our foes.

The hungry ravens flapped and fled,
From butchered streets where Crauford passed.
The women wailed around their dead.
Thin children shrank from us aghast.

Milord Cornwallis round us closed,
His noose was tight, his net was flung.
Horse, foot, and cannon well disposed.
The game was played, the trap was sprung.

Strange minstrels roamed from fire to fire,
Beguiling for a while the rebels' dread.
Yet nowhere did I find my heart's desire,
Or know the splendour of a vision fled.

I sought by mountain-side and fen,
A countenance I never found,
In hushful glade and haunted glen,
A song, a voice, an ossianic sound.

Oh, lack and longing cannot cease,
Jusqu'à ce que la longue journée finisse . . .

"Bold Sarrazin is gone and many slain.
No glory now in all this useless fray.
For this lost cause, why must we strive in vain?
Why must we," Humbert cried, "throw lives away?"

Oh, had I been the leader, moi,
Pascal François Tristan Dubois,
Of men that finished king and queen,
Soon, soon we swept that island clean!

"This is not how we fought at Quiberon,
Or slew the country lads in La Vendée
This is not how our slaughter fell upon
The ci-devant we smashed at Savenay!"

"Why must our courage ebb away like sand?
Our force is in the headlong dash!
No men are we to hesitate or stand!
Our fury is the lightning flash!"

Yet seasoned men stood firm and still,
While slaughter flowed on Shanna Hill.
Sardonic Humbert marked that hell,
That since Vendée he knew so well.

"Why do you stay", cried I, "you helpless band?
With pike and empty gun can you prevail?
Against this cannonade you cannot stand.
This grape, this canister, that lash like hail."......

"Why do you hold, you gallant few,
Your wintered hedge of sullen steel?"
"We only know that this is true.
Too deep we've bowed, too long we kneel."

"Come, follow me, brave hearts of France!"
My sword of wrath burned in the sun.
"And we shall lead these dogs a dance!
And finish well what we've begun!"

"Mais, suivez-moi, braves coeurs de France!
Such odds as these we've seen before!
Our Honour hangs upon this chance!
One fearless man is worth five score!"

But three - no more - advanced with me,
And may their names remembered be -
Bodel . . . Saint-Clair . . . and Jean Le Maure . . .
All, all are dead . . . Ils sont tous morts.

Invincible until we fell,
Le Maure, Saint-Clair et Pierre Bodel,
We surged against the English host,
A little wave, a granite coast.

The smiling Redcoats laid us low.
Into the night I longed to pass.
For two died quick, and one died slow,
And one lay broken on the grass.

How long I lay, I cannot tell,
All motion gone, my strength undone.
But English surgeons finished well,
What English muskets had begun.

In Dublin town they used us well,
In Dawson Street where we did dwell,
Regaling buck and demoiselle,
While rebel prisoners lived in hell.

In Dublin town they loved us well.
Fine fancy ladies came to see,
In twittering and fond farewell
Their gallant Sons of Liberty

who, hangdog, gay, knew well that they
Would live to fight another day,
Save Teeling, bravest of the brave,
A traitor now that none could save.

Teeling, de tous fidèle ami,
Face à la mort, tête haute, hardi.

Teeling, of all my faithful friend,
Head high and fearless till the end.

On Arbour Hill did Teeling swing,
A traitor to his German king.

Equality and Liberty!
Fine words that once meant much to me.
Equality, absurd and vain,
Where Bourbon kings obscenely reign,
And Liberty is cold and dead
To helpless cripple in his bed.

Give not your life, jeune homme, je prie,
To venturings across the sea.
Do not your life and love mis-spend.
Too soon all foolish dreams must end.

Soleil se couche, soleil se lève.
Douleur profonde n'est nullement brève.
The sun does rise, the sun does set.
My sorrow deep is with me yet.

I am very much indebted to Thomas Flanagan for his magnificent novel "The Year of The French". It tells the story of General Humbert's belated landing at Kilcummin Strand, Mayo in 1798 and of his final defeat.

The novel is told in a range of styles and from several different viewpoints both Irish and English but the soldiers of the small French force scarcely come into the forefront of the action. I therefore invented Tristan Dubois, who seemed at one stage of my poem to break away from me and follow his own strange tempestuous path. Though, looking back as a helpless embittered cripple on the whole tragic experience, he tells a young man who has asked for his advice to stay away from the attraction of military exploits..

"Give not your life, jeune homme, je prie,
To venturings across the sea.
Do not your life and love mis-spend.
Too soon all foolish dreams must end."

The story is far-fetched but the advice is sound.

THE KINGDOM OF LECALE

Repository of source and shrine, mosaic of name and lore,
That knows the past, the ambling quirk, of many a rambling way,
Grey lough and lake and gorse-gold hills, John's Point and lonely brae,
Encirclement of stones aware at ghosting of the day.

Below the hill where Patrick stands, frilled isles confront the shore.
Wave-white the pillars of the field where flows the ripening grain.
While, once, by rath or dolmen, or was it souterrain,
Came intercept of otherness from lilacs drenched with rain.

Sweet hiss of hedge and winter sedge in marsh that is no more.
Imprinted dream by cairn and cross where passed a steadfast man,
That claimed and held for centuries the hearts of chief and of clan.
High laughter of the herring girls that gutted cran by cran.

No bulwarks guard this realm of Lecale.
It has no No-Man's-Land, no wall, no pale.
No earthwork runs from coiling Quoile to Clogh.
No men-at-arms stand sentry in Killough.

And even here they pullulate, such souls as feast on fee,
That huckster fame and legend, the freehold of the sea,
The hallowed hills of history, the nearness to the strand,
Profaning ancient sanctities, clear well-springs of the land.

Yet, come what may and come the worst, the glories of Lecale,
Its hush bequeathed, its quiet airs, its ancient spell abide,
Persist in bell and prayerful cell, tower house and waterside,
Resurge on strand and furrowed sand, a salt and timeless tide.

PLAISIR D'AMOUR

They wandered by the ocean side,
Where wavelets lulled and marram sighed,
And in her heart she murmured, I'd -

In the golden autumn of the year,
When love was tinged and trapped by fear.

Yet staunch as earth, as seed sincere,
They came at length to here, to here,
Where I and I'm had turned to we're -

In the golden autumn of the year,
Though love was dark as mountain mere.

Soon, children hied and mothers cried
To see the blushing groom, the bride,
That oftentimes and side by side -

In the emerald springtime of the year,
By shadowed valley, slough and swamp,
Saw marigold both far and near,
Allume for them her golden lamp.

THE TOAD

In summers in the house of Bois Picard,
Within the orchard valley of Garonne,
Cicada drowsing in acacia grove,
Bucolic grumble of the oxen car,
Wine fields enriched by funding of the sun,
Plum-peach-pear byways I would rove.

The house was harvest, frame of mind, and hoard,
Full store of print and etching, souvenir,
Of art and image, rustic feast and dance,
Mankind and nature fashioned in accord,
Of fête galante, of rapiered chevalier,
Of Beauty's smile, self-loving in her glance.

No portraiture or picture, triptych, painted glass,
Forewarned me of
The toad.

I rose, once sleepless, from my columned bed,
Passed through a beaded curtain, almost stepped
Barefoot,
Upon the toad.
Clown-visaged clot of slime, gargoyle of lumpen clay.
I stood and stood, transfixed by disbelief.

The toad
Blot-bloat on silver brushwork of the moon,
Struck dumb the midnight chorus of the grass.

In crouch of condamné, submissive, weak,
It seemed disposed
To what I might inflict.
I shuddered back the life
I could have closed.

"C'est idyllique là-bas", the vicomte said.
Perhaps the toad,
Pustular, mendicant and meek,
In heritage of earth unfit to speak,
In stillness knew the idyllique.

*In the 1950's I spent three summers in the home of my friends
Pierre Recourat-Chorot and Daniel Mauny in the départment of
Lot-et-Garonne in France. The ugliness of the toad was a shock
in comparison with all the beautiful and artistic things that filled
their home. But it is the toad that I remember most clearly and I
can now understand that, in the eyes of its Creator, it may well have
conformed to some ideal of beauty far above our own.*

BETHLEHEM

In Bethlehem at break of day,
I heard a weary shepherd say,
"I cannot rest, I must not stay.
One sheep of mine has gone astray."

Thus did a learnèd shepherd say,
In Bethlehem at noon of day,
"A time to sing, a time to play,
Rejoice and wonder and to pray."

In Bethlehem at close of day,
I heard a wise old shepherd say,
"In that poor stable where he lay,
We saw the Life, the Truth, the Way."

LANDSCAPES OF THE MIND

Minutely I remember,
The house where I was born,
Where, June or live December,
The sun arose each morn.

I found Jim Hawkins' Benbow Inn,
The wreckers' shore, the smugglers' lough,
And Spyglass Hill dublooned with whin,
One scooter spin from sweet Killough.

I soared above the backyard wall
Upon a rope-and-cushion swing,
Saw rivers and trees and dustbins and all,
And socks and frocks upon a string.

In wild, forsaken, deep-sea grief,
The Merman called his little ones,
From rock or reef about Kilclief,
Where Strangford's tidal torrent runs.

In circling stones at Ballynoe,
Bold Patrick spoke with faith aflame.
One shining sky, not long ago,
Re-made that very day he came.

Far from Luftwaffe's strafe and strife,
That churchyard was my plot of play.
It was for me a field of life,
Invented by one Thomas Gray.

By Lagan stream where lilies bloom,
I loved the Lady of Shalott.
Though sigh of sedge, high toss of plume
Kept telling me that she was not.

THE TREE

"But there's a Tree, of many, one,
A single Field which I have looked upon . . ."
  William Wordsworth
    "Ode on the Intimations of Immortality"

I wandered lonely in a crowd,
Took pictures of the gardens and the guests,
Olympus-happy, roamed, explored
Parkland of ash and elm and leafless oak,
Each one complacent in its portioned space,
But battle-bared for winter's long campaign.

I looked at many, contemplated one,
That sheened the light in bark and bough and twig,
Upraised a column rooted as a mast,
Staunch bole that sprang from clay to pencilled art,
Spread wide its twining curves, complexities
Of grace that knew its purpose and its power.

A family joyous on long-shadowed grass,
Strolled with a dog that woofed around the tree,
As if it would not, could not, stop,
Accomplices of pleasure and delight.
I took some pictures, kept, of many, one.

Five years have passed.
I was, in each, no stranger to the tree.
A wrench of limb, steel frost, ampute of storm,
Have not impaired its growth, its will to live.
It knows nirvana, wakening, flourish of new leaf.
Its allocated span exceeds my own.
Its strength, its armoured resolution, outdoes mine.
It is a mystery, presence, and a thought,
And, changing for the seasons, touches timelessness.

Deep solace comes from image that I made
Of autumn scene in shining circumstance,
Of special treeness captured for all time.
Unvanquished still it stands, I know.
It signs defiance to inconstant skies
Its seeds, warm-bedded in the quilted earth,
Await the songbird wooings of the Spring.

IMAGE AND LIKENESS

I showed no wound. It was the blast.
I was a tourist in Belfast.

I was a nurse in Vukovar.
The shells came screaming from afar.

They broke my fingers and my back.
I was a shepherd in Iraq.

I lost my life. I dared to pray
For human rights in Mandalay.

My bowels burned, my brain was tar.
I was a bride in Kandahar.

They cut my throat from ear to ear.
I was a mother in Kashmir.

Chatila camp was purified.
I was among the throng that died.

I was a teacher in Kabul.
That bomb was smart. It came to school.

They loved my gentle eyes of brown,
A Spanish child in Omagh town.

I was an orphan in Algiers.
Interrogators shed no tears.

I drove a bus in Galilee.
He killed himself, five men, and me.

The fragments tore me limb from limb.
I was a babe in Bethlehem.

I took three hours to die my death.
A man that came from Nazareth.

TO MY FATHER

By block or counter, it's a long, long while,
You tended shop that could be cold as ice,
Your apron smudged and striped, your sharpening steel,
Your expertise in sirloin, brisket, veal,
Long knife in hand to cut and deftly slice.
Yours was the word that made the people smile.

The double doors were always open wide,
In premises more windswept than the street outside.
Long days and years you stood, no mollycoddling then.
The meat was more important than the men.
You chopped and parcelled, joked and smiled.
I smell the sawdust, see the walls blue-tiled.

Then quick as blade your wit, your repartee,
With customers from Cyprus, Cullingtree,
From Baker Street, the Loney, and the Falls,
From godly homes in shade of godless walls,
From Panton Street that owned a pawn,
From Lemon, Peel, and Cinnamon,
From streets an empire's conflict made,
Like Balaclava, Inkerman, Belgrade,
From Ross and Willow, Massareene,
From names that will no more be seen,
From English, Scotch and Theodore,
From Raglan, Milford, many more,
From Alma, Spinner, Christian Place,
Small worlds replacement would efface.

Your passage from the working day was gladdened by acclaim.
You knew the grocer and his wife, they greeted you by name.
Remitted from the treadmill, you held your head on high,
Enlivening each encounter with every passer-by.
- An' who's that big lad, Harry, an' tell us what's his name?-
While Harry here, and Harry there,
And Harry almost everywhere,
From doffer, docker, doorway dame,
Proclaimed (I thought) your everlasting fame.

Now, I was proud of you when I was young.
Though never rich, you found your pearl of price.
Too soon the evil days were come, the silver cord was loosed.
And now much older than you ever were,
I praise because in memory I am your millionaire,
And sing those kindly bygone streets because I loved you there.

CREATION

I met the goddess Ceres at Versailles,
Familiar on her plinth, familiar and serene,
A harvest wreath about her brow, her gaze above
Beau monde and sans-culotte that August day.

What art instilled so long ago, what sacred spark,
Brought forth, I mused, this replica,
Eternalising country-girl or proud marquise,
Creating semblance of my mother not then born,
My mother gone two full decades before,
I saw the goddess Ceres at Versailles?

Should I return, no Galerie Des Glaces,
Nor fountain, park, nor doleful Trianon
Shall lure me from
That contemplation of my childhood set in stone.

But, go or not, I still believe and hope,
That I shall see my mother's face again,
And in the cool of evening we shall walk
In gardens an immortal Sun King made.

ANNABEL

My thoughts that day were caught by looking at
Old Annabel, her ever-wobbling hat,
The earnest, ceaseless bobbing of her head -
Oul' prayer-machine, that's what the people said.

Half-hid, eyes closed, and on her lone,
To ritual oblivious as a stone,
What was her inner world, her frantic need,
That had no call for plainsong, book or bead?

I marvelled long what this might be -
Some language higher than the liturgy?
Recital of her pains, her thanks, her fears?
Some ecstasy distilled from bitter tears?

At solemnising of some major feast,
I slipped, inquisitive, to hear her least
Of word and whisper, find some quick insight
Into the force that drove her rapture and her flight.

She neither thanked, implored, nor made complaint,
Nor called upon some fashionable saint.
Long list she rustled, swaying, names she knew,
Like Annie, Aggie, whizz whizz, Paddy, whizz whizz, Hugh . . .

Her litany prevailed, she over-rode
The anthem, rubric, and the canon code.
Name-trove of all that she had loved or known,
She set before an altar and a throne.

My river hastens to a timeless lough.
I have my own, my private, whispered, stock.
One single name (that said) I now may tell -
Old-fashioned.   Long-remembered.   Annabel.

IDYLL

Rose petals incandesced upon
November beds the morn they met.
Dumb-struck, with memories beset,
She smiled, unloved, her sway long gone.

I'm new, he grumbled - he was old -
Oh, when you roamed high hills with me,
Whoever thought we both might be
Imprisoned in this fatal fold?

In corner of some sombre shed,
(Dead leaves that scuttled on the floor)
Pale dreams they sought, poor words they said,
Were fragments of their nevermore.

SAN JUAN CAPISTRANO

An afterworld, a sainted world, lives on by Capistrano,
In pillared close of cloister, oasis, El Dorado.
Beyond the candles and the gloom where fire-tongues flicker yet,
Cool-glad beneath their lily-pads, the gliding carp forget.

But intimation murmurs still of things not fully gone,
Of sword and benediction, of cross and morion.
While, reaching for a sky of blue in incandescent air,
The candelabra cactus and the palm aspire in prayer.
Grey lizards pulse like little sins upon the burning stone,
And the litanies are ended, and a dream is overthrown.

Remember, Junipero, this place you loved so well.
Hear your joyful children calling, hear the anvil and the bell.
Hear the vesper and the plainsong, and the soldiers throwing dice,
And the flowing of the waters in which man is quickened twice.
Behold, this day, your alcazar, your work, your sacrifice.

Set free from stern endeavour, your spirit turned to Spain,
But wings to Capistrano when the swallows come again.

WEST CIRCULAR

Creased carpet of the hedgeless fields and lanes.
Below.
Adventure enclave, Arizona sun,
Buttes, canyons, gulches, tessellated clay,
A desert-world, licked clean, a canyon that
Brick-hungry Belfast made.

Ceramic soil and tinkling shale,
Apache walls with gypsum veined,
Baked boulders on the oven floor and tin-foil leaves
Of plants that had, in Ireland, died of thirst.

Caught-breath and silence terrified our tread.
Tracks, bogies, crumbling timbers, sighed
Of miners dry-gulched, arrowed, gone. This was
The tumble-weeding West pre-tasted, seen,
Encountered fifty years before.

Above,
The legend over-spilled the pit.
The asphalt factory was a log-walled fort,
The loanin' by the Springfield Dam, a lonesome trail.
While from brick houses of Clovelly Street,
They scanned the green prairie,
 For men with eagle feathers in their hair,
And crimson circles round their ponies' eyes.

The Springfield brickyard - or claypit as they would call it in America - has long ago been filled in and the site is now occupied by a large industrial estate. But in the 30's and 40's it was a wonderland and playground especially since it was so evocative of the deserts seen in old western films.

By a strange turnaround the deserts of Nevada and Arizona when I did see them many years later were reminiscent of the Springfield brickyard so I thought that the name of the West Circular Road would be particularly appropriate as a title for the poem.

BRÚ NA BÓINNE

They dragged their griefs before me, moaned
Of lives and laughter lost, men pulped by toppling rocks,
Men rancoured by sore burdens of their toil,
Men robbed of rest, men crippled, drowned,
Men used like beasts that do not know the ends
For which they tug and strive.

They counted crops unreaped and cattle strayed,
Lambs left unguarded from the fattening wolves,
Rain-rotted shelters where their children died.

I sorrowed with them, drove them on.
I was the instrument and not the cause.

It was not I that ruled but dreams' torment,
Ancestral dreams, dreams born of ancient dreams,
Grim enterprise of bygone times,
Great forests hewed to mark the sacred hill,
To craft the levers, poles, the rollers, rafts
That battled with the river's sinewed coils,
Stone lifted, trundled, pushed and rolled,
Old imploration, history, love, belief,
Inscribed in everlasting sign,
And then

Dream-trusted lodging for our chosen dead,
Its caverned roof-stones tight as scales,
Where He would come.

And narrow vestibule and whirlings of the sky, the stars,
And circlings of all human thought incised in stone,
And mount of turf and stone that had no start, no end,
Round image of that living round of fire,
That sinks and seems to die in ever-shortening day,
But would, as faith affirmed, return again.
I fanned the dream to flame, the chosen shared with me,
Made light of bruises, dangers, death,
Found strength
Above their nature and all thought.

And I remember well
That night of nights grown long and longer still, that night
When men give way and feed upon despair.
We stood or leaned or shrank or shook
In blackness of the dark
That pressed upon us, choked the heart,
Made hope and expectation drip
As from some fearful wound.
No seep of light, no spark, no breath of dawn,
In blackness that amazed the sight, and then
A greyness that was guess and wonder, definition.
Oh!

He came.
The Shining One.
He arrowed whitestone portals we had made,
He shouldered up and up his brilliant way,
He strode from stone to stone, he entered as a king,
Into the chamber where we sobbed or knelt, or wept or cried.

He was,
All thirst of flesh or seed, all spin and thrust of life,
The infant at the breast, leaf language overhead,
Juice berries children fetch, red salmon in the stream,
Sweet apples on the tree, rich udders plump with cream,
High-autumn feast, much winter bread, the lilt and love of spring,
Sharp smoke of ash that guides the hunter home,
Long patient summer evenings and their aching peace,
Slow sigh of golden barley swaying its decease.

This was his pledge, clear as his flood of light,
That cold and dark and fear were done,
That He would rouse the sleeping earth,
Make green the living spears where we had scratched and sown,
Make grasses grow to feed the thriving herd,
Make birds and trees and waters sing.

He beamed upon
The dust, the ash, the shards of bone,
Or those that were confided to his care,
Encradling all the persons they had been,
To sail with Him on boundless seas of light,
And live forever in the Higher World.

He'd come, as I foretold, the Shining One.
I had no need, no more, to mourn my dead.
I pressed my trembling palms, my brow,
Against the stone that He had sanctified,
And lost myself in warmness of his touch . . .

Oh, I am old and very old, my kin,
Four times as old in years
As fingers on these knotted hands and soon,
A scraping of small bones and cinders must await
Another dawn.
But, brothers, friends, posterity,
He came at point of day and He will come again,
To inundate the darkness of our minds,
And linger gently in this ever-new abode,
That you and I have built for Him.

YOUNG WOMAN OF THE ROADS

Old Mary Brogan, grown grossly fat
Sank, day by day, into a horsehair sofa that
Became a black cilice, a penitential rath
For one that knew too well the primrose path.

On rare and rarer times she sprockled forth,
And, fortified, returned,
With scapulars and medals, holy pictures, books of prayer.
For she, like you and me, was infinite, complex,
Had tales untold, strange flaws, unbeknownst cracks.

Yet still from time to time, she would intone her songs,
Old ballads stiff with sinfulness of yore,
With waywardness of those that will not stop or stay.
The, soon, she'd pray
And call, God Pardon Me, one hundred times a day.

Remorse or no remorse, she was a dropout from
The family Rosary.
She rambled and collogued
With persons of the roads,
She lived cavortings, escapades and jinks,
And mumbled of her private mysteries,
Her Glories, Sorrows and her Joys . . .

Her first-born Gerald told me once
About the fierce young woman that would disappear,
And not be seen for months,
Until the peelers packed her home again,
To be once more the mother of an ever-growing brood
That could not hold her.

She never said where she had been,
And Johnny never stooped to ask,
As if their schism had not yet begun,
As if she was a treasure scarcely won,
As if her sins had not his love undone.

It was a thing that happened in those good old times.
A dancing folly, would you say?
Or else, a virus in the blood?
So many, men and women, just took off
From hovels, pogroms, scrape and scrounge,
From blazing berserk of the Belfast streets,
Mortality of mills that choked the lungs with lint.
Morality of pulpits hard as flint . . .
It was a choice they made, a lifeline and a flit,
Beguilement of the thrush against the factory horn,
The shackles of the streets unlocked by madness of the morn.

The homeless road, the crossed horizon, were release.
The given crust, the running stream, were peace.

Some stranger came before the end,
Some scrawny sibyl with long tatty hair,
Smelling of human nature and red wine.
It was October's end, the ebbing of the tide,
And Mary Brogan sang the night before she died.

They buried her one half a world away.
Her first-born Gerald did, he paid for all.

Thin weeping of grey plover ghosted all the shore.
Dead grasses massed by unremembered mounds.
Strange vagabonds upon tin-whistles thrilled,
To celebrate the tipsiness of flight,
The message of the moon, the dreamscapes of its light.

I'm sick of grubbing money, Gerald said.
My mother loved this spot, she came here many times.
She knew what's what, she lived her life for life.
She was herself.
(That Rambling Annie there, she told me things I never knew.)
It was tall summer when they found this place.
They screeched because the gulls were free as they.
They giggled half the day, they jigged in evening sun.
Don't talk about my father, good or bad.
He never tore himself in two, he never was alone . . .

She cried for me all day upon that stone.

THE SMALL HUNGER

It wasn't often Thumper stooped to praise,
But this is what he told the Head one day.
He may have seen Wee Jimbo twirl an' dance
An' score a goal,
Or trounce a bigger boy to show him what was what.

"A tight wee lad."
That's what the teacher said.

It was the year he left the school for good,
The year Old Thumper whacked them through this play,
That left the tight wee lad a bit nonplussed.
(Why couldn't Shakespeare write like anybody else?)
Still, there were lines he caught
And found cause, later on, to call to mind.
"If you have tears, prepare to shed them now."
And that comeuppance bit,
"These many then shall die; their names are prick'd."

And there was one that stuck
Like chewing gum on wellie boots,
"He was quick metal when he went to school."
He took it, as you might well say, to heart.

In that mean quarter where he scraped a life,
The metal cooled and cracked and flawed.
He quit the library when schooldays were done.
No time for stories any more, for make-believe.
The sports page kept him going and this set
He bought dirt-cheap in Smithfield, "Know the Game."
Football and Snooker, Horses, Dogs and Darts.

Real things,
Were pride and passion, laughing gas.
Beribboned cups for LIVE -ER- POOL
Were milestones on his downward way.

He had no more the urge
To venture forth, explore.
Dundonald, Ligoniel, Mallusk, were foreign names,
Like Paris, Moscow, Saskatoon.

The last name, though, he knew too bloody well.
He had this girl that went to Saskatoon.
"A better life," she said.
"A place where you can see the sky."

It was arranged.
He would go soon and they would meet,
An' tie the knot in Saskatoon,
An' have a house an' boys an' girls in Saskatoon.
In Canada.
He wondered sometimes if he'd ever see the place.

"I met, dear John, " she wrote, "this fella on the boat.
He looked like Gregory Peck."
The letter scored his heart.
His name was prick'd.

That finished him with Women.
He never liked them from the start,
Nor never knew what they were at.
Renouncement was a kind of peace although
He was quick metal when he went to school.

Big Richard always said,
"Your horse comes in, you buy a bottle, have a laugh.
That's all there is."

Big Richard knew the score.
And then the married men
That haunted Hooley's Bar were payback of a kind.
Their wives got all the rancid names their tongues could hold.
Like targe and tinker, trollop, clart,
And more,
Like whore.
An' whinge an' yap all day it drove them out the door.

He went to Bangor once with all the lads.
The sea was sad.
It splintered on the rocks.
He stuttered B-B-Betty, heard
A screech of gulls.

Back with the lads,
The bottles warmed the cockles of his wit.
He drank to quench, he never fluffed his lines.
He was the champ that made them all guffaw.

He Knew the Game.
He was quick metal when he went to school.

He died as he had lived.
Untended, hungered, and alone.

"A turn-up for the books!" Big Richard roared.

Gob-struck,
His mates in Hooley's fought to come to terms,
Found black profundities in pints of stout,
And called him Chuckles, One-Off, Friend.
And Hooley's till rang out a merry knell.

Do not regret the life he lost.
Deplore the lives he never knew.

THE BALLAD OF THE CHILDREN OF LIR

Around your castle walls this night,
The bitter blast does rave and ring.
Approach, good masters, ladies bright,
A sad and wondrous tale I sing.

You tremble now to hear the moan,
Of Aoife, demon of the air,
Of Aoife, cursed and ever lone,
Of Aoife of the streaming hair.

For she it was that long ago,
Espousèd Lir one smiling day,
And loved a while step-children four,
Finn Guala, Conn, Fiacra, Aedh.

But Envy soon, that sleepless Fiend,
Of Eve that died and children four,
In darkness of her heart did groan,
In blackness of her soul did roar.

They hate most deep that first loved well.
They sin most foul that never fell.

"Arise, Finn Guala, daughter good,
To see the king, your father dear."
"I dreamed a dream last night, last night,
Now, now, I dwell in mortal fear."

"Fear not, Finn Guala love, nor stay.
To Derravara Lake we'll fare.
I prize ye all as were my own.
And ye shall laugh and linger there."

The sun from down a smothered sky,
On squinted waters, strange, did pour.
"Dear children, let us rest a while,
And sport beside yon gallant shore."

In icy waters mountain-fringed,
They paddle now for childhood's glee,
While she in jewelled hand does hold,
A twisting branch of evil tree.

"Finn Guala, Conn, Fiacra, Aedh,
This Curse I cast on ye to-day.
Ye shall no longer children be,
But swans for time and times to be."

"Three Hundred Years by this cold shore,
Three Hundred Years on Moyle's grim sea,
Where sunset fades Three Hundred more,
Till One shall come to set ye free."

No small ones now to laugh, to play.
Sad, silent swans that drift away . . .

But who is this that lights from steed,
His voice upraised in doomful dread,
His anger dark as thunder cloud,
His noble stride, his kingly tread?

"Where is my lovely Finn Guala?
And where my splendid sons all three?
Ah, hast thou done them hurt or harm,
Deservèd doom shall fall on thee!"

Then from the waters of that mere,
He hears a voice, soft-sounding, low.
"Behold us now, our father dear,
Enchanted creatures, white as snow."

In vain the wretched Aoife cries,
And vain for mercy does she sue.
"Beg not, kneel not, thou monster vile!"
He draws his sword, her limbs to hew.

But Finn Guala, though sore at heart,
Heard yet the mother, took her part.

"Slay not thine Aoife, let her be.
For she has left us voice and life.
She once was kind, remember still
She was, some years, thy loving wife."

"My daughter pleads, thy life I spare.
I curse thee Demon of the Air.
I, Lir, pronounce thy sentence meet.
The Cloud shall be thy Winding Sheet."

Uplifted hands, O fearful art!
And Aoife hangs on high, on high,
Unworthy of the constant earth,
She falls into the screaming sky.

He reels, he sinks, upon the ground.
His tears spring up, an ocean tide.
In thrust and throb of pain he cries,
On bended knee, the lake beside.

All anger spent, and smitten deep,
He hears his children-swans that sing,
More lovely than the minstrel's air,
Or bird of dawn on climbing wing.

Then, rushes whisp'ring by the wave,
Sad rustling leaves on hazel bough,
Forbear the usage of their sound.
Entranced they listen, silent now.

Soft song they hear of running free,
Of meadows where a child might roam,
Of rath and hall, of stream and tree,
Of dancing flame, of pleasant home.

"Nine hundred years we must abide,
By lake and sea, and ocean side."

Deep-wading by that stricken shore,
In broken voice now hear him say,
To swans that swim to father's hand,
"Finn Guala . . . Conn . . . Fiacra . . . Aedh."

Upon an island in the lake,
He builds a shelter from the wind,
And mansion by Devarra's edge,
Where all they loved they still might find.

Each dawn the children seek the strand,
Each day good friends exalt their fame,
While bards and scholars, poets too,
The sorrows of their lot proclaim.

But time destroys, and men forget.
Kings wither, die, and swans live yet.

Four orphans mirrored in the lake,
By roofless ruins softly glide.
Behold them by that lonesome shore,
Alone in this lone world and wide.

"Long, long, the life of pine and yew.
Slow, slow, the seasons' ebb and flow.
But longer still, and slower too,
This mournful questing to and fro."

"Do not despair, dear brother Aedh,
Though all we loved have passed away.
Far, far away, a deed is done.
A ransom paid, a victory won."

Three hundred years are lapsed and lost.
The spell prevails, the children go.
On sorrow's wings, they pass above
The brambled halls of long ago.

Deceptive Moyle beguiles their pain,
With lap and murmur of her sea,
With web of gold upon her sand,
With glint and gleam in all they see.

But soon, the swoop and howl of gale,
The hiss of sleet, the sting of hail.

Poor banished creatures, horror-tossed,
About those bitten walls of stone,
Seek room in vain along that shore,
More black than sin, more white than bone.

To wooded streams that wind the vales,
They dare not go for rightful fear,
Of watchful men that lie concealed,
Of men that hunt with net and spear.

A rock became their dwelling place,
One rood of green where they might lie,
Half-shielded by a ridge of stone,
But bruised by sea and scourged by sky.

The furies of the bounding wave,
Again, again, did boom and crash.
The very rock beneath them writhed
To cruel whip of lightning flash.

In solace of her wings she folds,
Poor Fiacra and trembling Aedh,
And gentle Conn below her breast,
And thus they bide till break of day.

And when at last the storms were spent,
She sang old songs of times gone by,
Of secrets that their father told,
And of her dream that would not die.

"When we shall hear a coming sound,
The tolling of a blessèd bell,
Then we shall be ourselves again,
And all things know and know full well."

"Nine hundred years with all their tears,
Shall be as they had never been.
They'll cease to flow, and we shall know,
A hallowed place, a rest serene."

"These agonies shall never cease,
From salt and woe, from storm and snow.
This Moyle will never be at peace.
It holds us, will not let us go."

Oh, watchful and death-fond was she,
That serpent-cunning, coiling, sea!

But one day came, ay dank and drear,
When evil tides begrimed the strand.
Four swans arose on draggled wing,
Observing Aoife's grim command.

Six centuries had swept across
The land, like floods upon a shore.
Their former scenes they could not find.
Their happy world was now no more.

Oh, vastness of the ocean sea!
Its wrinkled range, so cold, so wide!
Its long horizon flat as death!
Its endlessness on every side!

Some terror grips their faltered flight.
Dead leaves, they spin, more low and low,
Like blossoms torn from orchard tree,
Infirm, they fall as whirling snow.

In tenebrous and muffled cave,
They seek the comfort of the grave . . .

"Ah, let us huddle here no more,
In horror of this final sea.
Take heart, my brothers, let us soar!
The royal blood of Lir are we!"

From higher than the falcon's flight,
Where cloud-ship sails in skies of blue,
They find beyond the churning wave,
Fair harbours where no wild winds blew.

For pounding siege had breached the land,
With tranquil loch and sheltered creek,
Raised ramparts that repelled the foam,
Made haven from the ocean bleak.

One island drew their grateful gaze,
Strong hills between it and the sea,
Lake waters, fruitful of repose,
And daisied grass, and upright tree.

Reprieved betimes, they sojourned there,
Snug-safe among the rushes tall,
And would have made that isle their home,
Were they not prey to cruel thrall.

But on salt grass by winter shorn,
Poor spell-bound creatures still unfree,
They shook to trumpets of the storm,
To silver stallions of the sea.

From spinning cliff or mountain tor,
Or dune or cape, or mirrored beach,
They, wistful, watched white birds that winged,
To far-off lands beyond their reach.

Poor waifs that knew nor kin nor friend,
This grief, they thought, might never end.

And ancient heartbreak would they sing,
To gentle seals assembled round,
Their dark eyes soft with sympathy,
Their hearts attuned to human sound.

For this, at least, they had not lost,
To hold converse, to sweetly sing,
Tho' thirsting for one human voice,
And for that word that it might bring.

Their banishment was almost done,
When to their sanctuary they sped,
And by the lake a stranger man,
A circled light about his head.

"My people true", they heard him say,
"Depart until this Easter-tide.
Some work there is that I must do,
In this lone isle, by this lakeside."

Concealed from dawn till close of day,
They caught the prayer that was his breath,
Against the sun with arms outstretched,
Like one that died a ling'ring death.

"He loves nor bread nor ease nor rest,
Nor costly garb nor strong abode.
But who is he, what his intent?
What does he bring, and what forebode?"

"Behold the man, my brothers dear,
That ends our hunger and our fear."

Four swans, four swans, all side by side,
On arrowed waters sailing slow.
He rises from his knees to bless,
Four swans, soft plumes as winter snow.

"Now, God be praised, I know you well.
His power is of eternity.
And He shall break this evil spell,
And here am I to set you free."

Long, long, he spoke with cross in hand,
Of One that died in far-off land.
" Now, Patrick is my name " said he,
"And I am come to set you free".

"I, too, have lived in servitude,
And tended sheep on Slemish Hill.
I stand for Iosa that said,
Of justice shall you have your fill."

Up from the shore, with bell and flame,
And singing soft, his nation came.

These found their human form, alas.
Consider them with piteous dread.
The summer of their age is passed.
The golden flower of youth is fled.

Four children, feeble, broken, old,
Their flowing hair more white than snow,
They kneel as once their father kneeled,
Beside a lake so long ago.

The waters shivered on their brow.
With claspèd hands they sweetly died.
He rowed them to their earthly home,
Where they might slumber side by side.

*   *   *   *   *

My tale is told, the fire burns low.
The anger of the storm shall cease.
Then, let us pray before we go,
That Aoife, too, may find release.

One wonder, though, that did betide,
For, on the closing of that day,
About the grave where these were laid,
While many wept or fell to pray,

The wide-winged flock, pure-white as snow,
Arose, arose, from earth below,
And higher than the eagle's flight,
Turned oceanward from coming night.

In glory of a Sanctus bell,
They passed into eternal day.
Cried Lir, cried Eve, that loved them well,
"Finn Guala . . . Conn . . . Fiacra . . . Aedh!"

MILLTOWN

By Milltown's front gate
Lie the good and the great,
Archbishop and boss,
Marble shrine, Celtic cross.

But God's Acres surround
A wild-meadowed ground
Stone thickets abut
On what seems uncut.

These fields are the tomb
Of the penniless whom
No carvings acclaim
For office or fame.

Dropped into wet clay
Until Dies Irae,
Pell-mell and en-masse,
Under gossiping grass.

In thousands they lie,
Poor as church mice, small fry,
Cheek by jowl, row by row,
In disgrace of no-dough.

These were the defeated,
The beaten, the cheated,
The slaves of the mill,
The inmates, the ill.
The destitute,
The underfoot.

By hallowed grasses walk with care,
Saints, sinners, and poor souls are there,
And humps and hollows, silent stones,
And living tears and clay-clad bones.

A child is here that had no shoes,
An' Maggie-Anne that pawned her shawl,
An' Daftie Dom that loved the booze,
Mad Miles that had no home a-tall.

And there a legal loser broods,
That got ten years for stolen goods.
Not far away two cobblers wait,
That got the boot for being late.

Here lie a mother and her three.
She loved right well but not wisely.
Here lie until they shall uprise
The lowly that the high despise.

But by the gate
The proud shall wait.
These pass before
The Monsignor.

PEACE

I have found peace,
In churches where the shawlies spoke to God,
In trolley-bus to hear the Dawning of the Day,
By frieze of winter trees, and strange to say,
From things outmoded, cross-grained, rambling, odd.

I have won peace.
In grief and loss, and, what's more wonderful, at times
When all around cried carnival.

I have discovered peace,
By oasis that from Mojave sprang,
In Crocknafeola Wood where winter moans,
From Angelus that through the Sperrins rang,
On English grass by Dovedale stepping-stones.

I have sought peace,
In verses hammered, grouted, stone on stone,
Small-windowed walls, seclusion, cease.

I have known peace,
In introibo of an interdicted rite,
In contemplation of the shepherds and the kings,
In welcome of green Spring's volcanic might,
From swoop and flash and swing of cloud-white wings.

I have gained peace,
In chat and clash, in lone and foolish dream,
By seemed-inviolate-once the Mountain Loney stream.

But I have been possessed, ordained, by peace.
I kept an infant in my arms,
Before a flame that made all shadows leap,
At darkening of the day.

ONE MOMENT GREEN

Warm-pillared beech, seat-banks of old-leaf gold,
Green-lyric field where sheep content in fold
Inclined as if in pilgrimage or prayer.
A threshold never to be found again,
In hidden, nameless, re-remembered lane,
Somewhere between Belfast and Ballyclare.

I might have known the meaning of those trees,
That breathing art, leaf murmur, proffered ease,
Been healed from howl of engine, hustle, hell,
From brazen blare of mad ferocious speeds,
Addressed that venue, met its mystic needs,
One welcomed guest in that entrance, that cell.

I stood, I stood, impatient to decide,
If I should hasten or, in trust, abide,
Green whispers wooed from all around, above,
To set aside the promise I had made,
Submit to cool enticement of the shade,
Forget my single self, be lost, and love.

High leaves for music and a ditch for seat,
A moss-green bank, a haven from the heat.
There leaned a wall in fronds of maidenhair.
There laughed the stream, the yellow iris bloomed,
And honeyed meadowsweet queen-crowned and plumed.
Clear as a glance, a smile, the invitation there.

I wish that I had seized that time afar,
Partaken of the stillness of the scene,
Had been, perhaps, what I have never been,
Had glimpsed among the leaves one single star.

I sensed it as I unavailing stood,
The now now now of some infinitude.

OLD MASTERS

You could have been eighteen the day I saw you first,
Forlorn, ensludged in adolescent gravitas.

Once, on a bus excursion, others played the fool.
I would have joined them but you leaned my way,
Expatiating on the Four Last Things,
Death. Judgement. Heaven. Hell.
(Cloud-galleons sailing by.)

I saw you twice in forty years.
Long-faced and earnest at some city dance,
More lonely than a cemetery tree.
The second time in Browne and Nolan's store.
You'd bought some jotters, crayons, posters for the wall,
Were half abashed at all that cash you'd splurged,
And nervous of the mob in Isobel's.

I asked a personal question. - Sadly, no!
The countryside was emptied, so you deemed,
The girls (you jittered at the word) were all In Town,
So from the Cares of Marriage you'd been spared.
Although you'd often longed, you must confess,
To have some children of your own . . .

And then, one day, your name was in the "Irish News".
A consummation that awaits us all.
I travelled with three men whose work, like mine, was done.
We sketched your days with chalks of long ago.
No one had known you well.

The Mass was long.
And from the words of pupil-priest that spoke,
I caught some echo of your ancient ways,
For in his sermon you were Mister yet.

Away, away, we leafed among
Flashbacks of memory blurred by speed,
Snapshots of college, work, decline, cold breath of death.
I mentioned that you spoke of Heaven in the bus to Saul.

The Doctor said at last,
(He'd been the most sententious of us all)
"Up there we'll be less pompous, so I've thought.
  Our turn will come to listen and be taught."

LOVE

My son is dead.
I have no tears to give.

They watch me, strangers now.
Yet pride upholds me still - conclusion - task fulfilled.

The drought will pass, the downpour come,
The void,
Cyclones of pain.

Eyes closed, a-sway, I shall recite his name,
When these, good-hearted, take their leave and leave,
Me with my grief.

(how small he is, so slight) . .
(he almost seems) . . .
(so light as when I bore him first)

-They talk of burden, little do they know!

Eight years, ten months, eleven days, I was his shield.
He never knew how people looked at him,
Nor glimpsed that hell his manhood years would bring.

He could not speak, or walk, or cease to salivate

and yet he loved
all, all that time,
and knew, because of me he knew, that he was loved . . .

Disfigured prince,
I held you in the palace of my love.

LEGION

I am the child the lion took I am the man
That tracked the creature, pranced upon the kill.

I am the one that swam to save, I am the coward on the sand.
I am God's troubadour that scolded Brother Wolf,
Or, greased with sin, the captain of the robber band.

I am of Hiroshima, Nuremberg, Culloden Field.
I store some ancient guilt, I wonder if I was the wretch
That fled the moor bereft of sword and shield.

I stumble, soar. Speak truth, and lie. Am silent, sing.
I am what most I dread and love to fear,
The leper at the gate, the scarecrow and the king.

From right to left I read. My tongue was made
To shape all sounds and utterance of speech,
To croak in caverns deep the mystery and the masquerade.

In bone and blood they clamour still,
Affinity, throwback, primeval will,
Genetic memory, myth, impulse for good or ill.

I am the species and the scheme.
I am Tecumseh Sherman burning to the sea.
His deeds are in me, tulip in the bulb,
Dry seed and dream.

IRELAND OF THE WELCOMES

(Air - "The Mountains of Mourne")

He stands long and lonely before he sits down,
A stranger alone in a strange Irish town,
A man with no job and no money to spend,
No home and no welcome, no helper nor friend.

Far away little children, his mother, his wife,
Yet he dreams of some chance of rebuilding his life.
For them, and them only, he came to our shore,
Now he's trudged every street and he's knocked every door.

It's a country, they told him, where poverty's dead,
Where the stranger is welcome, so the stories all said,
Where the jobs are aplenty, the livin' is high,
An' the man that works well is the man that gets by.

Now he isn't from Antrim nor Carlow nor Clare,
Nor Dublin, Dungannon, nor plains of Kildare.
His name may be Stefan or Jozef or Jan.
But imagine, one moment, he's Paddy or Dan.

He might be Croatian or Polish or Czech,
Just imagine he's Irish, that time has turned back.
Your fore-fathers, once, sailed the dark lonely sea,
Met the cruel and the kindly.   Which one will you be?

LAZARUS

I am become
A stranger to all men and to myself.

All aimless as fireflies in river dusk,
Winged memories flout the crying of my soul.
By olive garden, sheepfold, nets upon the shore,
I stop, stop dead, upon some brink
Of recognition then my sisters,
Martha, Mary, bring me back
To trouble me with questions though
All words are vain
And cannot hold the things that I have known,
No more than hand may cup the evening star.

While scorpions sleep in torment of the day,
And jackals howl for dark, I cannot rest,
Who knew the blessed avenues of death.
I sink into the night, I long for God-knows-what,
For Word that holds all music, answer, speech,
For Friend ascended, gone, beyond my mortal reach.

By lilies of the field, I weep alone,
Remembering raiment brighter than their own.

MOTHER

Within the kindness of your womb, I dared to dream,
That I might know the fullness of the light,
Might be your sprig of hope, your soul's delight,
Might, with one infant smile, all pain redeem.

I loved so well the love within your voice,
That, previous, cried (permitted to rejoice)
My rose of all the years, my ever-precious one,
My shrine, my pledge of life, my daughter or my son!

Sly counsel intervened before my course was run.
For you had human rights and I had none.

A thing unborn, an end that had to be?
They err.
 I was.
 I am.
 I live eternally.
Yours, yours, the loss.
Whichever way you turned you found the Cross.

Weep now no more. Accept no sad despair.
I am your own. Look forward as before.
Wait patiently until
We join again.

My Mother dear,
Both now and evermore,
The child that you relinquished loves you still.

LA ROSE DU SABLE

Black columns by dead seasons petrified,
Prone obelisks calcined when forests died.
Slow wingless scarab on a grill you crawl,
And dream of May, starred meadows, waterfall.

But now by dune and burning stone,
Lost caravan and pallid bone,
This is your own.

Your oasis,
Where wanderings cease.

You've known mirage, strange booming of the sands,
Sore slip and trudge, sad-blistered heart and hands,
Here is fresh glory of full-fronded trees,
Abundance, lotus, quaff, and dappled ease.

From depths unfathomed and unseen,
These are your waters, sweet, serene
From what has been.

Your oasis,
Your Golden Fleece.

Too soon, above, away, the moon rides high.
Long vagrant breezes in disquiet cry.
In love's constriction you have known your fill.
Moon-spell commands. You know you must, you will.

Goodbye to shade and shadowed floor,
Bright coins of sun like louis d'or,
Brimful the pool, the parting shore.

False was your oasis,
That promised peace.

Your desert will not let you stay,
Its fearful stars, the furnace of its day.
Unmerciful the thirst, the famine and
Some say the wind cuts roses in the sand.

*In the Sahara desert the wind has its own artistry, makes strange
shapes in rock and sand. According to legend it may even carve out
in uncanny detail a rose of sand, a fleeting image where no garden flower
could possibly exist.*
*But this poem isn't just about the desert. It's about human
relationships, of our restlessness, of the shifting sands of our fidelity.
I myself treasure, from Algeria, an authentic sand-rose which was given to
me by a very dear friend. It is hard and enduring, unlike most human
relationships.*

THE FAIRY FORT

One railing pulled back like a capital D,
A push and a shove, from the park I am free.
The fairy Fort beckons, on, onwards, we pound
To green ring of its ramparts, our own holy ground.

Primroses by millions, gold blaze of the whin.
Mad roars that were music, bad words that were sin.
Our morning was ever, to hell with regret.
We galloped and fought, made smoke signals and yet

Asprawl, betimes, upon the breathless grass
(We held no faith in fairies or their lore.)
We counted clouds like histories that pass,
Reversed the time-tide, rambled years of yore.

We imaged sentries on the ramparts' edge,
In clay beneath the brae a crock of gold.
Horn-helmet devils in the hawthorn hedge.
The rath was mute.   It never told

Its end or origin. It's gone. So long.
Where, where? The city's there. Rath, fortress, dún,
And what it held of rite or wrong
Scraped clean. By brass and bully and buffoon..

"Things dead and gone are never worth the fuss.
What did those people ever do for us?
This land is ours to use and domineer."

They danced by the light of the dún, the dún,
They got, gave life, and we are here.

LOVE STORY

Foul Winter had played false the Spring,
With wind that cut like assegai.
The leafless ash, the lifeless land,
Forbad to love though not to lie.

No fervour then in all that scene.
Too blind the snow, too blank the sky.
One word in imploration raised,
Would lose itself, as April die.

Yet in that iron waste they heard,
Some phantom of some tinkling sound.
They followed it to where a rill,
Inscribed its windings in the ground.

Snug-sheltered by its eaves of ice,
That fondled and seduced the light,
A lilliputian river flowed,
In sun-warmed swirlings of delight.

They saw a tiny pebbled beach,
A pool where waterboatmen fared,
Cascades so bright as long ago,
As morning songs they once had shared.

One moment then they dreamed to roam
The shores and shingles of that rill,
Where waters gleamed and sparkled, where
Remembered summers trembled still.

But, banished from this kindly land,
Disbarred by self and solitude,
Alone, alone, though hand by hand,
So near and yet so far, they stood,

And saw within that spangled stream,
The danse macabre of their dream.

VIGNETTES

From time deceased, I browse the leaves
Of pleasures I have known, their brightening of
The dull nightshading of our age,
That sees nor cloud nor clover, wanders blind
To all that is not pelf, or pictures in a box.
These are my silver coins, the brilliants of my mind . . .

The Grey Man's Path a-shiver in twilight.
A crannog island sinking into night.

A bronco moon
That rode the daisied prairies of the sky, sunbeam
That painted resurrection on a Gothic floor.

Thrill-fear of reckless solitude, a howl of snow
That passed in strange and frightening hush,
And creviced wall and stunted thorn
Where weariness was peace, and stillness joy, and hungers met.

Trees toppled for my rest, grass bowl for dog-tired drowse.
And oceanful of bells, of blue bluebells, ring, bluebells, ring,
About the whitethorn trees.

And meadows hummed with sleep, soft murmurs of the sea,
Salt breath and waft of weed by billows hurled onshore.
Clear stream that bubble-danced in fresh encroaching cress.

And scent of woodsmoke, living fire,
In tabernacle of a hollow tree and wonderment
Of comfort, laughter, primal shelter from
Wolf ravening of the wild winds overhead.

And setting-out of boats in fog of Lough, their moans
Of boldness or of woe, their wishful faith and mine
When all the world was there and wide.

And halting place, one day, when light revealed
The never-random art of heather, shale and stone,
While instantly
Each granite grain, each curve and swell and dip of Mourne,
Was population, presence, word.

And only once a grove of hilltop trees
Where self-marooned one world-long day,
Lightfoot on 1940's leaves I lost all else,
But fortress, Little Bighorn, coral isle.
And all around, around in sweet Tyrone,
Patch-quilt of hedge and field where small birds sang.

Millrace of memory brings,
Stone gateposts, symbols of an art no more.
Crab-apple tree in shelf of stream,
Kingfisher flash too swift for cry's delight,
Wheat-fields and stiles and evening bells,
And lands unfenced where happy children played,
And fuchsia blossoms, red as World War Two,
And pathways, lanes, cart-rutted roads,
And things that ticked like watches in the grass.

I have not listed all, but am content to see
These leaning towers above a drowning land
Resist the swill and sluice of time,
Take tint and definition in my rhyme.

THINE IMAGE DIES

Across the baseball pitch, he called and called my name,
As if he held some right to interrupt our play.
Shamefaced and slow, I left the gang, the game,
If not for him, for coin, at least, for silver coin, that might repay.

Reclusive, proud, in tittle-tattle street,
He kept himself aloof, had neither chick nor chil',
Forlorn, they said, yet to himself complete,
Responding (only just) to neighbours' greeting or to smile.

I watched the family grocer, slice, and slap, and pour.
Unhurried hands that revelled in their art.
"Ham, butter, sugar, tea."   He winked.   "That's four and four!
He must have struck it rich, your Mister Harte."

His door was unsecured.   "Come on on in! I'm over here!"
A twinkling fire, tobacco scent, steel fender gleaming bright.
And books , old cherished books, tier after tier,
His deep armchair, his softly-shadowed light.

Imagined futures lead the mind of youth astray.
I dreamed myself, in time to come, in such array,
From sink or swim of life, ashore, away,
And happy with such tomes the livelong day . . .

I had no notion then of how it might have been to hear,
In fruitless age, strange children's cries around,
And surf of breaking laughter in an empty room.

But now, with friends and family richly blessed,
It is in less fortuned I see the sadness of the self,
The pain of moments lost in time's old cunning tilt,
Of things that should have been and never were,
Or never more can be, and then the sore, the sad,
The swiftening misery of that last and lone glissade.

NOVEMBER MOON

Columbus of a newfound world,
One time beyond my mortal ken,
From meeting, throng, and randyboo,
I fled the masks and masques of men.

Soft airs, full moon and cloudless sky,
By bare-back hills I came to where
My Tiger Cub, my silver steed,
Ran Strang Fjord roads from here to there.

Grey Abbey, tucked in bed, grey streets from traffic free.
(How sweet the moonlight sleeps upon that bank!)
Glim-glitter on a Zuider Zee
And road and roof and leafless tree.
Gloved, hatted, happed, I lapped the swan-road sea.

And, as we purred along, along,
I hummed some snatch of silly song,
Persimmons on an ivy tree,
My little engine sang with me
Of Bishop's Mill and Walter Quay.

Beyond the quiet town a dreamsome world.
A ship that slid the strait with sail unfurled
In silvered seas upon the tide.
Moon-lantern pathway joined the other side.

So much of that one night, of all my years
Is lost. Nor fret nor strive nor tears
Illuminate the deeps of what is left behind.
I set, in meagre verses, fragments that I find.

ADVENTURE

I could stand here for all this longing day
To contemplate this prospect, quiet, old,
The stream that through the meadows runs astray,
The distant hill ablaze with gorse of gold.

One time too far, one time too brief,
I could not, would not, be so still,
But thrashed and crashed through thorn and leaf,
And rambled freely at my will,

And leaped the stream with thoughtless ease,
And trampled over sheugh and flowers,
And wandered idly as the breeze,
Nor marked the mad impulsive hours.

Then fished with pin in running brook,
Sought sky-blue eggs in grasses tall,
Explored each lair, each shadowed nook,
Thrilled to the lapwings' lonely call.

And, from the summit of that hill,
Have seen, with palm to shade my eyes,
Famed Samarkand or walled Seville,
Have thought the world my toy, my prize . . .

But why stand still until the set of sun?
Or in cool twilight lost in reverie?
No lads about these fields will ever run.
Or sway the topmost branches of that tree.

TREK

I roved the Long Mountain and Blaeberry Hill,
Outdistancing chorus, compulsion, treadmill,
Knew laughing of water, caressing of air,
Whirpooling of bubbles, rotundas of air.

I squelched in sponge moss, I plashed in black mud,
Recoiled from a torrent combative in flood,
Rotated in circle of summit and cairn,
Trudged wetly by bracken, bog cotton, green fern.

Came mischief of storm, swift malice of sky,
Battalions of deluge where nothing was dry,
Drum-rolling of thunder, remoteness that quailed,
Whiplash of the arctic, steel pellets that flailed.

I envied the smartness that stays in the street,
Dismissive of mountains, of misery and sleet,
I prayed for warm shelter, the flame and the fry,
Loud voices and song, tall stories forby.

But fierceness passed, the sky was swept,
By winds of grace less chill.
In alb of snow a summit slept.
Two streams conversed beside a hill.

In cloister of a granite wall
(Red-berried ash gold-leafed and tall)
I knelt with chaliced hands to drink my fill.

STRONG FJORD

The map says much.
Long finger of the Ards, contact withheld
From thumb that is the Kingdom of Lecale, and there
Upon the tip, deep-bitten by the sea
A blunted nail, and there, between,
Between Killard and Ballyquintan Point
The entrance to the Lough
Taut as a bow, a lough to launch
One thousand little ships,
A world enclosing worlds, a world ordained to be
Insurge and inspiration, scrolling of the sea.

And memory tells
Of this strong fjord,
What line and tint and letter cannot show,
Salt-splash of little gardens made
By flower and stone, by rocks with gold inlaid,
Lough murmurings like robes upon the grass,
Green mirrored isles upon a lake of glass,
Meandering shores where haste and hurry cease,
Twine roads that saunter to the sea's caprice.

And this, on either side, was real, was true,
Unique, supreme, unparalleled,
This residence of sanctities, infused, unseen,
That lived in grass and water, strange accord,
A stillness he perceived
More keenly than myself -

I mean the one that went with me,
To visit ancient walls of abbey stone.
We were eighteen, the parting of the ways,
We walked by mudflats, foreshore, rising tide,
Held high converse, as young men do, of life
And years ahead and choices to be made.
We came to windows pointed as a flame, conflict of rooks,
And were abashed to silence that the place distilled.

He moved, he sat apart, arms folded in his sleeves,
To rest, it seemed, to ponder and to pray,
And made his choice, I do believe, that hour, that very day.

Along the trudge of our return
(The August evening torched across the sea)
He never voiced the dream he had, and now afar,
He crowns a life I cannot guess or share,
A life of cloister, work and prayer,
And he shall walk our onetime way no more,
But has his stronghold on a better shore.

I have been told
That he remembers, still
I must not go
To cast a ripple in the full-tide of his peace,
Or stir the waters where he finds increase.

DELPH DOGS

They dwelt for a time in a jumbely street,
Where peoples and creeds and mythologies meet,
Put up pictures of Lourdes and a statue or two,
Of God's Holy Mother in mantle of blue,
And china dogs, lop-eared, above the fireside,
P. Pearse and Pat Sarsfield, installed, satisfied.

Two spinsters set free from their sad years in school,
Found peace and contentment in timeless capsule.
They cherished a message they had from the Queen,
And photo of Father who died at Messines,
And china dogs, pop-eyed (King Charles) in a nook.
The first was King Billy, the next Basil Brooke.

Platoons of poltroons at the family's front door,
Told them that they couldn't stay there any more.
They fled with their bags and their traps and their woe,
To the overturned trucks of the nearest ghetto.
The house was dismantled, it must be confessed.
And Sarsfield and Pearse were kidnapped in jest.

The claymore went off as the soldiers passed by.
The roof of the sisters arose to the sky.
They clung to each other in terror and shock,
As CRASH down the stairs came the grandfather clock.
Their windows were shattered, their curtains were tore.
And Basil Brooke busted his arse on the floor.

Time passed as it must and here's where they've been,
The one in an attic, one in a shebeen.
They met face to face in the Cancer Research,
King Billy and Sarsfield upon the same perch.
Delph dogs were the in-thing, they were the whole-go.
They fetched a fine price and the sale wasn't slow.

Now they live in L'Derry with all kinds of junk.
Their owner's befuddled and mostly he's drunk.
He's taken a shine to them both equally,
Especially when quaffing his evening chablis.
But when he's asleep and a-snore in his bed,
King Billy and Sarsfield are never quite dead.

THE FRUGAL MEAL

In hallway of a home that time undid,
In pictured monochrome, penumbral hand-to-mouth,
A den where light itself was underfed,
The Frugal Meal.

Non-light ungenerous and obscure,
No plates or forks, no saucers, cups,
No knives.
Just spoons,
Spoons and the bowl,
And hunger, hunger, all around,
And spoons circumferential to
The Frugal Meal.

Pinched forebears smiling at the bonus of the feast,
Thin children placid in their common lot.
Enough was (this was then) enough.
Long spoons,
To dip and sip, to scratch and scrape,
Each scrap
Of gruel, stew, dilute panade,
Of mash of cabbage, turnip, bean,
Until the bowl, the turner's second best, was clean.

The Frugal Meal.
A strange extension grew,
The more you looked at it.

Frugality.
A word that died,
Dissolved in jet contrail, consumed by acid rain,
Along with others moribund,
Like justice, truth, commitment, sin.

The meal was frugal for they never had
Baguette or gateau, applecake or Bakewell tart,
Sirloin or fillet, bacon, jellied tongue,
Or kipper, salmon trout or Dover sole,

Or Port-Salut, Red Leicester, Brie
Or double cream, French Fancies, Zinfandel.
(I list the goodies that I know too well.)

Frugality.
The word is buried in a nettled grave.
Dead now, the virtue, mode and pride,
That was
The Frugal Meal.

The old ones passed, of spartan fare perhaps.
The young survived.
The breed is overfed and boisters in the streets.
The grandsons wear long knives upon their way
To the buckets and troughs of the Big Butt Café.

TIME LAPSE

O darkling years post World War Two,
When sins were black, hearse-horses too!

When cobble-stones were glazed with rain,
And skies were pallid, pewter-plain.

When grass was charred and roses grey,
And Sunday was the Sabbath day.

When hucksters' shops were dark and small,
And tattered bills hung from the wall

When everything seemed bleached and bare,
And corner-boys would stand and stare.

But cuties sauntered on the prom,
In colourful and chaste aplomb,

While gentlemen of better class,
Took photographs as they did pass.

They knew the ropes, they pictured well,
Give them their rightful due.
But monochrome could never tell,
What teenage vision caught and knew.

. . And caught when girls were green and fair,.
Pretending that the boys weren't there,

When butterflies, chromatic, bright,
Were Painted Ladies of the night,

When Heather blushed on ardent hills,
And June got blitzed on daffodils,

When trams were mad-electrick-blue,
And popsies painted like the Sioux,

When Amaryllis decked the hall,
And lady birds tripped to the ball,

When dogs peed on the lampost red,
And ginger cats turned pink and fled,

When daisies blue and violets white,
Splashed Fifties meadows with delight,

When rainbows fluoresced each street,
And black-and-white came obsolete,

Then Kodak, Agfa, Fuji too,
Sold for a song, the full palette,
Of colours, undiluted, true,
Defining vision's boundaries, yet

Some still see what they want to see,
Deep in darkrooms of memory.

TRANSITION

That terminal summer of Nine-Forty-Three,
White beauty of blossom, maraud of the bee,
When mushroom of Love was in brew like the Bomb,
They collogued in the shade of the maidenhair tree.

Though Paper Doll sang outside the nuns' gate,
These lassies conformed and did burningly wait.
They whispered and giggled of pleasures when from
That long garden path they must soon graduate.

But now they are weathered and old, ochonee,
Grand-mothers of mothers and mothers-to-be.
Tart-bitter and sweet was the fruit of that tree.
And living was seldom what they did foresee.

CLONARD CONFRATERNITY

The Monday congregation was urbane,
Vexilla sectioning the crowded pews,
Stern prefects graced by register and chain,
Gold-ribboned veterans floating off
On avé wavelets to some blameless shore.

An old-world sermon. Which may well have been
Upon some virtue or some pious rite,
Or sins that silver heads abandoned long before.
Quite often, though,
Lives Of Old Saints that more than once began -
"He was born in the little town . . ."

I pictured to myself,
A city-citadel upon a hill,
Hugged tight by stonewalls and by certitude,
Crossbowmen crying buon viaggio
To friars of fortune, girded, good . . .

Then, incense, candles, benediction, bell,
And prayer bequeathed from some intemperate age -
"For members out of town . . ."

For members out of town?
What could this be?
It seemed, that time, extremely odd.
Did lawless men abound in County Down?
Or wolves infest the hillsides of Dundrod?
Could there be highwaymen in Portavogie town?
Or tigers on the road to Tandragee?

One final hymn and then
Outside,
So many that were dying for a smoke,
And asked politely for a light.
The little flames sprang all around,
Portents
Of rituals to come.

Odd now that none could then foresee
The night when flames would roar
In little homes in shadow of those walls.

MY KINGDOM FOR A ...

'Longside the train on hill or plain,
    I am a wingèd horse.
With might and main and flying mane
    I hurdle hedge and gorse.
With wings endowed, light as a cloud,
    I trot my summer sky.
I vault the town, I float down, down,
    Don't ask me how or why.

    You'll speed up in vain,
    You silly old train,
    Tho' faster an' faster you go.
    My race I'll maintain,
    My pace I'll sustain,
    By orchard and church and scarecrow.

On fields of June in sleep of noon,
    I skim the springing corn.
I stride the lane, outride the train,
    all obstacles I scorn.
I sail aloof above the roof,
    the thicket and the thorn.
To clack of wheels, to brakeful squeals,
    here comes the unicorn.

By sheugh and by swamp,
    I tread and I tramp.
By banks of the burn,
    I twist and I turn,
By places just made
    for rest in the shade,
Resistant to lure,
    such things I abjure.
I laugh and I leap
    where motorways creep.

I jump over quarry, dark mountains an' corrie.
O'er streamlet an' stream, an' gardens of dream,
An' forest an' farmland an' chattering brook.
The moorland an' funfair, the wild an' the free,
Are revel an' rout to Pegasus me.
Oho, the big river, I'm out on the Spree!

By gate and estate and mansion ornate,
By freshet and spring where bushy birds sing,
By trees of sun-slant where new leaves enchant . . .
But here comes a town,
Where my train must slow down.

By desert and highland and steppe and savannah,
By acres of spuds and square miles of banana,
By gardens of praties and looping liana,
By tundra and alp and steam-jungles I've passed -
But here come the streets and the stops of Belfast . . .

Oh, slowly, slow, he leaves the train.
He walks with stiffness and with pain.
But will, in dream, skyhigh again
From piggyback train, back, back, to Coleraine.

EIGHTEEN

Averse from evening's fearful scene,
I meet myself when I'm eighteen,
And, as a curly cabbage, green.

Ensconced upon my time machine,
Above the lad I once had been,
That other-self of long ago,
That ever-primrose-path-bucko,
That candid cluck without a clue,
That April muggins, ingénu,
Palaeolithic next-of-kin,
Anachronistic semi-twin,
I thunder till his hair is curled
Upon misdoings of the world,
Bestowing till I'm puffed and hoarse
Buckshee advice none can enforce.
I wheeze that life is hard at best,
And there's more pain than love or rest.

Upon his face a giddy grin.
He cannot, will not, take it in.

Astride upon my saddle-tree,
I eye the lad I used to be.
But is this HIM?
Or is it ME?
How dare that madcap vis-a-vis
Degrade my name so callowly
Why was he programmed from his birth,
To search for what is not on earth?

But fellow-feeling saves the day,
Why did I launch this strange foray,
Against this soul, tight-buttoned, thin,
This also-ran, this harlequin,
Scared stiff by Brutes that Boomed of Sin,

Bewildered, hot and cold in turn,
Worked-up as an electric churn?
I must assure him, if I can,
That life has Meaning . . . Measure . . . Plan.

He will not listen, that I know.
On his deluded way he'll go,
Dismiss me with some jejune jest,
Believing he alone knows best.

I almost call him back and say
(But that would give the game away)
You shall, testator of my years,
Bestow on me your songs and tears.

No bridge is there across the sea.
With time and tide we cannot plea.
Though eighteen will not come again,
I've learned a wheen o' things since then,
And written with a goose-quill pen.

WILD FLOWERS

The poorest flower that we can find
Spendthrifts a wealth beyond our mind.

**It cannot make me rich, therefore,
It is a weed that I abhor!**

Alas, that we must bid adieu
To Cowslip and to Primrose too.

**Exterminate the meadowsweet,
That useless thing I cannot eat!**

The smallest child that goes to school,
Knows Buttercups are beautiful.

**Come, merry maid and laughing boy,
Destroy, destroy, the traveller's joy!**

Enchanter's Nightshade, cast your spells,
On acolytes of toxic hells.

**Come poison stream or acid rain,
I'll sell my soul for further gain!**

In summer breeze, O sweet Harebell
My pilgrim weariness dispel.

**The fragrance of the wild woodbine,
You may not breathe for it is mine!**

To country girls whom they should wed,
The Ragged Robin long has said.

Cleanse all these mountains, let's begin!
Incinerate the worthless whin!

Loose not the chartered philistine
Upon the Lesser Celandine.

For clink of coin my land was sold.
Ah dinna prize yer marigold!

Our Mother Earth, of flowers devoid,
Shall not renew what you've destroyed.

INJURY TIME

In inn
Rude voices ruled, tobacco smoke was dense
As denizens. The bar was wet
With tears unshed.
Basso profundo howls
Made virgins wonder in the rain
Outside
If there was something they had missed.

In inn
Mad whoopings for the clobbering of the foe.
And beery bonhomie.

In inner world,
The pain
Of loving offered, taken, fouled, and kicked offside.

In inn
High fives of mate to mate, swing, lunge and kick
To emulate the glories of the goal.
An' drink up quick, there's none in hell, wee man.

In brain
The pain
Of match abandoned, lager-logged terrain.

He'd spent too long, he thought,
With ignorant gulpins could split their sides
At bleeding of a mate.

But hatred was relief,
Like blows and bruises to be given,
And received.

WISH YOU WERE HERE

The bad men came to our wee house.
It wasn't long ago.
But why they did that wicked thing,
My Mammy doesn't know.

We heard an awful bang downstairs,
At once we all awoke.
An' everybody wondered why
The room was full of smoke.

Our Daddy wasn't there, he's dead.
But Mammy's wise and strong.
She lifted Baby from his cot.
It didn't take her long.

She counted us, two, three, four, five.
She broke the window frame.
She set us on the scullery roof.
I heard her call my name.

We huddled close together there.
The rain was falling fast.
I didn't worry 'cos I thought,
Someone will come at last.

They brought a ladder from next door.
An' up came Mister Brown.
He held us tightly in his arms,
An' carried us all down.

He was so brave, he saved us all.
Polly and Jane and Sue,
Our Mammy cried for joy an' hugged
Wee Tom that's only two.

This woman took us in her house.
She wrapped me in a rug.
She gave us hot cross buns to eat,
An' chocolate from a jug.

The fire-brigade arrived on time.
Police an' soldiers too.
The amb'lance had a big blue light,
An' made a noise would frighten you.

I sat beside the amb'lance man.
He told a funny joke.
I told him what my doll was called.
My Mammy never spoke.

They put us in this great big house.
You call it a Notel.
The chicken pie was very good.
It had a lovely smell.

An' later on we got the bus
To Auntie Bethie's door.
She's got this great big gorgeous house.
It's right beside the shore.

We hear the waves in bed at night.
We paddle in the sea.
We gather sea-shells on the beach.
An' Polly plays with me.

We've tons of chips three times a day,
An' sausages an' things like that.
We eat like horses, Auntie says.
An' Jane is getting fat.

I want to stay here all my life,
An' never go to school.
It's awful warm, the sky is blue.
We love the swimming pool.

We're happy here with Auntie Beth.
Our old dog Jack got burned to death.

SANS MERCI

I capered round some France of long ago,
And fluent as the river Loire is long
And rich as Creosote, bought for a song
The mirrored chateau-bridge of Chenonceau.

The language was no problem as before.
My eloquence was vaunted far and wide.
Where once they stood perplexed and mystified,
They shouted, "Bis!" - In English, that's "Encore!"

I told a bold gendarme to be begone.
I ranged the Cévennes Mountains with an ass.
I trampolined upon the Mer de Glace,
I floored a waiter with the cry, "Garçon!"

I was the darling of the Boul' Michel.
They marvelled at my braggadocio,
My jeux d'esprit, my crackerjack bons mots.
I told Louis Quatorze to go to hell.

He is a lionheart, I heard them say.
No pain or danger will that fellow dread,
For he on honey-dew has fed . . .
Too soon they found that I had feet of clay.

*　　　*　　　*　　　*　　　*

Red-brick of castle in pure evening's light.
Pleached alleyways for dalliance and for dance.
And demoiselle of incandescent glance,
That gazed upon me with such dark delight!

Her beauty hit me like a blunderbuss.
My knees were rubber and my spine was sand.
I was undone, uncouthie, and unmanned.
I realised I was one cowardly cuss.

She wenched my lion's heart away.
I almost swallowed my pince-nez.

My courage ran like melted snow.
I turned away both tail and toe.
I took French leave of machismo.
I fled to Chicken, Idaho.

ENTR'ACTE

The job was done, we wanted out-out-out.
Two hangers-on were we that liked to roam,
Just muscle men that shifted props and flats,
And loved the chorus on the late bus home.

We'd seen the play ten times or more,
The slap and sally of its kitchen wit,
The senile shiver of its frail decor,
Its humour of the earth, the slurry pit,
The tuppeny convolutions of the plot,
The deep and lovely things that it was not.

We left the street, found inundate of light,
Clear sky as backdrop to the rising moon,
By shadowed miles we rose, we passed on high
To balcony, to gods, above
One silent tableau, thralling as a dream.
White cottage, lamplight, shining stream
One silvered shallow valley where
The world was breathless as a prayer.

It was a one-night show, we knew it then,
This empty stage, unscripted mise en scène,
This hushed prologue, its Aphrodite due,
This summary of want, its overview.

Each locked in lone surmise,
We stood long - longing - in that interlude,
Then paced in stillness, down

To tea and buns and chat and bus.
And never spoke about that cabaret,
Or saw each other much, each on his separate way.

They tell me now,
He played on the banks of the River Meander,
And learned to curse
The cheap theatrics of the moon.

BIRTHDAY

It is not being old that hurts the most,
Nor quickening trickle of my mortal sand,
Nor tremor of the long blue-rivered hand,
Nor weakening of the will to best and boast.

I shun the pane that mimes my painful stride.
I am not moved by beauties of the dawn.
I learn indifference to the glance of scorn.
I march no more with promise by my side.

Where are they now, companions, that walked the earth with me,
That knew the famine of the stars, the thirst that is the sea?
Disbanded now and burdened, some broken, many dead.
O daisy-chained chimera, O bruckle, brittle thread!

I mind the tents of laughter, songs we sung.
What hurts the most is this ,
All earth - immortal earth - our borrowed earth - was young.